A Handbook of Natural Rights

Life, Liberty and the pursuit of Happiness

Dan Wolf

If you purchased this book without a cover you should be aware that this book is stolen property. It was reported as "unsold and destroyed" to the publisher and neither the author nor the publisher has received any payment for this "stripped book."

A Handbook of Natural Rights

Copyright © 2018 Dan Wolf. All rights reserved, including the right to reproduce this book or portions thereof, in any form. No part of this text may be reproduced, transmitted, downloaded, decompiled, reverse engineered, or stored in or introduced into any information storage and retrieval system in any form or by any means, whether electronic or mechanical without the express written permission of the author. The scanning, uploading, and distribution of this book via the Internet or via any other means is illegal and punishable by law. Please purchase only authorized electronic editions and do not participate in or encourage electronic piracy of copyrighted materials.

Cover designed by Exodus Design Studios

Printed by CreateSpace

Other books by the author:
Do You Want To Be Free
Collectivism and Charity
A War for God
Coexist

Visit the author website:
http://www.livingrightly.net

Other articles by the author can be found at:
http://www.vachristian.org

ISBN: 978-0-998756-74-5 (eBook)
ISBN: 978-0-998756-73-8 (Paperback)

Version: 2018.08.12

To God. I pray I have been, and will be, a faithful servant. And to my wife who has endured endless hours of conversation and requests for her opinions with my writing. If not yet a saint, she must be well on her way.

There are two ways of looking at the pattern of human activities which lead to different conclusions concerning both its explanation and the possibilities of deliberately altering it. Of these, one is based on conceptions which are demonstrably false, yet are so pleasing to human vanity that they have gained great influence and are constantly employed even by people who know that they rest on a fiction, but believe that fiction to be innocuous. The other, although few people will question its basic contentions if they are stated abstractly, leads in some respects to conclusions so unwelcome that few are willing to follow it through to the end.

—**F.A. Hayek**

Table of Contents

Introduction	i
Chapter 1: Rights	1
Chapter 2: Being	25
Chapter 3: Actions	55
Chapter 4: Dominion	93
Chapter 5: Implications of Human Rights	119
Notes	149

Introduction

My search has led me to the simple belief there is no freedom without faith and that freedom is a gift from God. When man turns away from Him, he will fail to realize that gift's benefits.

This fifth book comes full circle, leading back to the first book's premise. *Do You Want to Be Free* explored the notion of freedom. Christ's teaching led to the development of societies based upon our shared nature, virtue, self-sacrifice, and self-reliance. The works of three early church fathers—Clement of Alexandria, Augustine, and Thomas Aquinas—provide different aspects of man's relationships with man and those between man and God in relation to freedom, and how those relationships translate into governance.

Collectivism and Charity outlined the actions and values we should see in a society realizing freedom's benefits, because they are on the right track. When man turns toward God, he places himself on a path of transformation, a path that leads one to becoming good. We become good by performing individual acts of charity, fulfilling divine law at the same time. Christ's words were not given to either the Church or State, but to us as individuals. Charity is our responsibility.

These first two books built the case for what should be in terms of principles, values, and governance and examines whether America's society is on the right path. The next two books look at corruptions of those relationships. *A War for God* examined Islam, an ideology like communism and socialism that springs from the same root—a root that is contrary to, and incompatible with, Judeo-Christian principles. The two cannot coexist. The differences were examined from the perspectives of culture, language, doctrines, documents, history, theology, and the attitudes arising from those differences.

The fourth book, *Coexist*, began by looking at how Islam has co-opted the interfaith movement toward its own ends, but also examined how that movement has been used to inject postmodern principles into religion. It represents a world where truth is no longer objective, but instead is subjective, with man defining his own truth and then constructing an echo chamber so he can listen only to those thoughts. This worldview plays itself out in many ways: trying to remove religion from the public square, erasing history, and espousing human rights. The book addresses the questions of how should Christians respond and whether we can still keep faith in such a society.

All of this sets the stage for *A Handbook of Natural Rights*. There seems to be endless talk today about our human rights. How society is to provide everything for us, and it will all be free—because it's all about outcomes. Such a view is intoxicating, but also sheer lunacy. In fact, it is sheer stupidity—the result of an education system run amuck that is more focused on ideological indoctrination rather than preparing its students for success. And that is why this book has been written. It is dedicated to all of those students our institutions have failed to educate in those things contributing to life's success. My hope is it will provide some small education on a topic that is critically important for them personally as well as the society they live in.

Education's failure places our society in grave danger, because we cannot succeed unless we know and understand truth and morality. Without those things, self-governance is no longer possible, and a case can be made that a people who've strayed so far do not deserve to govern themselves. But it doesn't have to be that way. The real power lies in us as individuals, but only when we are turned toward God as His people, a single people with a common set of rights and a shared commitment to the common good. This cannot ever come from any government program, for it is our responsibility. We can abdicate that responsibility, but we will still be held to account for it in our final judgement. And whether you believe that or not doesn't matter. I can believe that if I jump off a cliff, gravity will not pull me down. However, that doesn't change the reality that anyone attempting such an act would plummet like a stone.

This book's purpose is to serve as both an educational piece and quick reference guide: an educational piece because the language of faith, and often today that of reason, is no longer taught in our schools. Many people of faith no longer study or read what they claim to profess. This work will point you in the right direction and at the very least give you some things to think about. The book is laid out around five distinct and easy-to-understand topics, using original sources wherever possible. I will not tell you what to think: You must arrive at your conclusions by yourself. However, I do believe the evidence to be very clear.

Chapter 1 examines the whole idea of rights. What are they? Where do they come from? Are there different types? Do our choices impact our rights? How do laws and rights differ? What is the relationship between these two ideas? These questions are used to define some terms and create relationships we should expect to see if we are on the right track. We then look at some of the ways man has corrupted these notions by examining some Christian heresies. These are used to derive some ways man has turned away from God in the past, because these ways are still used by those seeking to corrupt society today. It is important that we understand them so that we will recognize them when, and not if, we see them.

The next three chapters begin by looking at God, creation, and man's place in that creation. What do we need to know about creation? Why was it made? Who is man? What is his place in creation and with God? The answers to these questions lead us into discussions about natural rights in the areas of being, actions, and dominion. A chapter is devoted to each of these three areas.

Underlying these rights is the notion of grace. Our natural rights were gifted to us out of love, and they should evoke a response of love from each one of us in return. This expectation of returning love for a gift we've received sets up a corresponding duty with each right we've been given. We choose whether to fulfill those duties or not, but our choice doesn't change the moral obligation we each have toward them.

Chapter 5 uses the material from the three previous chapters and flips that material on its head to showcase how man has historically attempted to corrupt these ideas—corruptions that go back to the same heresies noted in Chapter 1. Nothing is new under the sun; man only forgets that he has forgotten. This chapter ties in some of the more significant collectivist claims we hear from our politicians, educators, media, and talking heads today. In case you do not know what collectivism is, you can just use the words *communist*, *fascist*, *progressive*, or *socialist*. They are all the same in this respect.

Their claims are all baseless, but with the repetition these falsehoods receive, they may begin to appear true. That is the problem with a lie. It must be constantly repeated or else the truth will begin to emerge. The chapter closes with some suggestions for how we can prevent ourselves from losing our way and at the same time stand for the truth. After all, that is what we have been called to do.

We are not born with any of this knowledge. It must be learned by each new generation so that it can be passed on to the next. That is the responsibility we owe our children. This is my small contribution to that effort. I pray it may serve you well.

Before closing, I would especially like to thank Jeff for his editing and suggestions, and Kris for the cover artwork. Their contributions served to greatly improve this final product.

Chapter 1

Rights

Why does the topic of natural rights matter? First, America's founders believed they were important enough to start a revolution over after they were taken away and all other avenues to restore them had been exhausted. Their list of natural rights vary as we discern them using our reason, but generally they included life, liberty, property, religious liberty, happiness, keeping and bearing arms, and the freedoms of speech, press, and assembly. Each of these are incorporated into the natural rights framework set forth within this book.

Second, natural rights provide the moral underpinnings for any and all societies. If they are not present, a society will not be successful in the long run because it will lack the necessary moral foundation for goodness and trust. Our founders believed in a Creator, but this is not a theological issue. James Madison wrote,

> The interest of the man must be connected with the constitutional rights of the place. It may be a reflection on human nature, that such devices should be necessary to control the abuses of government. But what is government itself, but the greatest of all reflections on human nature? If men were angels, no government would be necessary. If angels were to govern men, neither external nor internal controls on government would be necessary.[1]

Madison's argument is if one being has the right to rule another without their consent, then that being must be infinitely good, wise, and powerful. *No man has these qualities.* Therefore, "there must be a natural right to liberty, i.e., a right not to be compelled to submit to another person's rule without consent."[2] However, while the existence of natural rights is not a theological issue, I will assert a society holding to and living Judeo-Christian principles will have an easier time understanding and observing natural rights than one that doesn't.

Third, you won't find natural rights taught in our schools today or discussed honestly in our media or by many politicians. There is an emphasis on "our rights," but silence on the duties that come with them or an outright denial of the latter's existence. Rights are expressed as "human," but they do not all come from the same source. Some rights are positive and others negative, but we no longer distinguish between the two. Finally, we act as though freedom grants us license to do just about whatever we want, and if someone doesn't support our choices, then they must stop doing whatever offends us. This notion is a corruption of freedom and natural rights. Government is not intended to be a club used against other society members. Each of these points is discussed later.

What Are Natural Rights?

This sounds like a natural place to start. What is freedom? What is a right? For this work, we will use the following definitions. Freedom is "the absence of coercion—to the extent that this is feasible in organized society. It means that ability of human beings to act in voluntary fashion, rather than being pushed around and forced to do things."[3] This provides a flexible framework that does not tell us what those things are, but at the same time one's freedom to act cannot infringe upon another citizen's freedom. Each citizen has equal liberty, which is necessary to prevent an individual or group, whether minority or majority, from becoming repressive. It takes the club of government out of the hands of those who wish to use it to control others.

Next, a right is *that which can be claimed on the basis of moral or just grounds*. It emanates from righteousness and is therefore grounded in virtue. If you want to realize the full potential from your rights and thereby live well, you must understand what they are, where they come from, and why you have them. This chapter sets the stage for those discussions.

Are all rights the same? I will argue that no, they are not. Some come from God, and some come from man. God, as creation's Creator, is its governor. He is infinite and has the power to create. He also has the power to change or end anything at any time. His claim is therefore superior to man's, as man was created by God—man is finite. Further, God willed things to be and they were. Man's creating abilities are limited to making things from already existing materials; man can merely transform something that already exists. Therefore, his creating abilities are also less than God's.

The natural rights God's given to each one of us are grounded in His unchangeable goodness. As Creator, He's given everything existence, and this existence is evidence of His goodness. For to be is surely better than not to be. His goodness is the source of all righteousness—morality—and therefore virtue. Man's created rights (human) are grounded in his changeable nature. Any rights God bestows on man must therefore be superior to rights created by man. His rights are timeless in that they are grounded in truth—truth that doesn't change.

Why Do We Have Rights?

The short answer is we were each given free will, the freedom to make—and responsibility for making—our own choices. This freedom is God's gift to each one of us, and we cannot fulfill our purpose without it. Those rights coming from God have their basis in His morality and support us in fulfilling our purpose. The rights He's provided allow us to use our freedom in achieving our purpose, *if we choose to do good*.

How this gift supports our purpose leads us into a discussion about grace and free will. St. Thomas Aquinas (Thomas) described grace using the example of the king's grace in his *Summa Theologicæ*.[4] All three parts must be present and in the order given. First, the king loves one of his soldiers. Second, out of that love the king gives the soldier a gift, one given gratis (freely). Third, out of this gift love is reciprocated from the soldier back to the king. It all boils down to love, what the Greeks called *agape*. Unlike a human king, who loves some of his subjects and others not so much, God loves all of His creation—each and every one of us. Otherwise, He would not have created us in the first place.

While Thomas wrote extensively on this topic, he relied heavily on some of Augustine's material written over 800 years before, in the early fifth century. It is to those materials we will look for answers, specifically, Augustine's *The City of God*, *The Enchiridion*, and *A Treatise on Grace and Free Will*. We'll continue this discussion by looking closer at our purpose.

Purpose

Our purpose is simply to become good. God made all of creation, and it was good. God made man in His image, an inward image, and it was very good. Man was created good.[5] Evil is the absence of good, the result of man's choices when he turns away from good—that is, God.

Accomplishing our purpose requires several things.

1. Holiness: Consecrate yourselves therefore, and be holy, for I am holy.[6]
2. To Know and Do: Everyone who hears these words of Mine and acts on them.[7]
3. Obedience: We are to exhibit the well-ordered obedience of faith to eternal law.[8]
4. Worship: We are to worship God in faith, hope, and love.[9]

This is not a complete list, but one highly relevant to the topic at hand. Grace is another of God's gifts, and evidence of His mercy. According to Augustine, "Out of His fulness have we received, according to our humble measure, our particles of ability as it were for leading good lives—'according as God hath dealt to every man his measure of faith'; because 'every man hath his proper gift of God; one after this manner, and another after that.' And this is grace."[10]

Grace is God's gift, including the skills, abilities, and aptitudes we each possess. These gifts are sufficient in fulfilling our purpose, and differ for each one of us. We therefore each fulfill this common purpose differently. Faith, hope, and love all support fulfilling our purpose, and there are several relationships between them we need to understand. Faith and hope have to do with knowing God, while love with doing as God has instructed.

Faith, Hope, and Love

A friend asked Augustine, "What is man's chief end in life?" He responded knowing thoroughly the proper objects of faith, hope, and love.[11] Faith, hope, and love are the means to that end, and are to be defended by reason, a reason that springs from

1. Our bodily senses (knowing creation);
2. Intuitions of the mind (knowing God's image within us);
3. The testimony of those witnesses who wrote the Scriptures (knowing revelation).

Faith is the beginning for hope and love. Without faith, these other two cannot exist.[12] Faith is belief, and it is concerned with the past, present, and future. Faith may have both good and evil as its object, because both good and evil are believed, but the faith that believes them is not evil, but good.[13]

But as noted above, faith itself is not the beginning. For Paul said, "I have obtained mercy that I might be faithful."[14] God's mercy is His freely given love to man: grace. This grace is given gratis and not based upon our own merits. But, even after one has become justified by faith, grace should accompany us on our journey, and we should lean upon it, lest we fall.[15]

Hope differs from faith in that it has only good as its object. It is the expectation of good things to come. It is the light that shines in the darkness. Hope is the basis for our actions and, unlike faith, it is concerned only with the future. Lastly, the virtue of hope doesn't change with circumstances.

Finally, love is what we are instructed to do: first to love God and then our fellow man. For without love, faith profits nothing, and in its absence, hope cannot exist. The Apostle Paul approves and commends the "faith which worketh by love," and this certainly cannot exist without hope. Therefore, there is no love without hope, no hope without love, and neither love nor hope without faith.[16] Love is faith and hope's fulfillment.

Thomas called faith, hope, and love the cardinal virtues, because each oriented us toward God. Further, the Greek word for this type of love—agape—is translated as both love and charity. The first translation refers to love's affect and the second to its actions. From these notions, along with virtue and free will (freedom) mentioned earlier, the following model can be derived.[17]

There is one additional item to add to this diagram, and that is peace. Peace is obtained when we become good through the happiness that comes from fulfilling our purpose and the obedience with divine law that comes from charity performed in love. This is true peace, eternal peace, and cannot be achieved without faith, hope, and love.

Why Choice Matters

The above model's qualities include some of Christianity's most basic tenets: God, grace, faith, free will (freedom), virtue, hope, charity, love, and God's law. These also underlie our country's founding principles.[18] We are not so much a Christian nation, but rather one built upon Christian principles. However, I would argue it is not possible for individuals, or a people, to achieve the end mentioned above apart from Christianity.

We all know people who personify the above model. They usually seem to just have a gift for the way they live. However, sadly there are many who choose not to live in the way just described, and some identify themselves as Christians. The Pew Research Center's *Religious Landscape Study*[19] indicated about 70% of the U.S. population claims to be Christian, and another almost 25% indicated they were either atheist, agnostic, or held no particular religious views. The remaining 5% were made up of other faiths.

Today's Problem

We look around today and really should be asking ourselves what's happened. We are a divided nation. Division does not come from God but from man turned away from Him. Obama was largely successful in leading us into a national transformation, but our leaders do not take us anyplace we are unwilling to go. He was a weak leader as he did not possess the qualities outlined above. That is not my opinion. It is based on his actions and their fruit. Racial tensions have increased and our law enforcement vilified to the point where some are shot. School shootings skyrocketed under his administration. Government corruption increased (see below). Hope diminished—yes, the hope essential to the preceding model.

Then there are all the scandals: Benghazi, the IRS targeting of conservative groups, the Fast and Furious program, and the lies told knowingly about Obamacare to get it passed—to name only a few. His abuses of power in enacting environmental regulations, defying court orders when they impeded his goals, and his administration's more recent apparent withholding of information to get at least one FISA warrant to spy on a political opponent—again, just to name a few. It is telling that the former President said, "We didn't have a scandal that embarrassed us."[20] He's right. They weren't embarrassed at all. The above are actions taken by a man turned away from God, despite whatever anyone may say to the contrary. The evidence speaks for itself.

But there is very good news. We can change course at any time, and that change starts with each one of us. When enough people put God first, then our leaders will follow and corruption will diminish. Why? Because there will be more faith, hope, and love, and we as a single people will be less accepting of the vice occurring when man turns toward himself, especially among those we choose to lead us. *That choice is always ours to make.*

Making Bad Choices

We can either turn toward or away from God. That is man's choice, using our free will, and we are always in one of those two states: either moving closer to or away from Him. The only time we maintain a relationship with Him is the brief point when we pass from one state into the other.

We've covered the alternative of moving closer to God in the preceding discussion. What about the alternative of falling away? This next section lists some ways man falls away from his intended relationship with his Creator, supported by Christian heresy examples. All heresies involve man limiting God in some way, and man thereby elevating himself. All have their basis in pagan thought. But these heresies did have one benefit: They sharpened Christian doctrine and man's understanding of God. It is no different today

Why does our relationship with God matter? After all, He wouldn't take away the rights He gave us, would He? No, He would not. However, if we aren't connected with their source (God), we shouldn't be surprised if our rights seem to disappear. But make no mistake, His gifts are still present, we still possess them. It's just we no longer realize their benefits as we are turned away from their source. The promise we were given is if we follow God, He would bless us. Part of that blessing is realizing the full potential of the gifts we've been given—the freedom, skills, abilities, and aptitudes we've each received—and effectively utilizing our rights in fulfilling that purpose. *When we turn away from Him, we lose that blessing.*

None of the following discussion is meant to disparage any group. This is not about people as today's liberals so love to assert, but ideas. *Ideas matter as they influence our choices. They shape who we choose to become.* The next sections review the facts about heretical beliefs present in falling away from God and why they matter. This material also stresses history's importance and why we must truthfully remember it if we don't want to repeat past mistakes. We never make any true progress solving a problem unless we are willing to accept truth.

How We Go Off-Track

So what are some of the ways man can turn away from God? They include

1. Denying God's existence;
2. Denying God's nature;
3. Denying Christ's divinity;
4. Denying Christ's humanity;
5. Removing Scriptures;
6. Adding to Scriptures;
7. Man's relying on himself:
   a. Grace received through our own merits;
   b. Rejecting grace altogether;
   c. Knowing God without doing;
   d. Doing in God's name without knowing Him.

Some Examples

We can put these heresies into a few broad categories. The first is the denial of God altogether. Other categories include Trinitarian, Christological, and Gnostic, all explained below. All spring from pagan thought, sometimes by very pious individuals trying to do what they thought was the right thing. Going much further in classifying them is fruitless as there is much overlap between them. In some instances, one heresy is the reaction to another and therefore could fall into several categories. This information was compiled from many different sources.

While many of these heretical ideas have been around for well over fifteen hundred years, most have modern-day counterparts in our culture. Don't believe that statement? Just pick up a magazine, go to a movie, watch one of today's talk shows, or pick up a self-help book and examine them in the light of what is about to be laid out.

<u>Denying God</u>

This is atheism, faith turned from God, faith that no longer has God as its object. This mode of living actually takes a great deal of faith, for to believe in no God in the presence of existence is a contradiction, as there is no other rational basis for creation other than God. And there is a creation: existence. Jean-Paul Sartre stated that the basic philosophical question is that something is there rather than that nothing is.

<u>Trinitarian</u>

The heresies mentioned in this broad category have to do with God's nature and power. We'll start with those about God's nature, specifically those concerning the Godhead's triune nature. These notions, and those in the next section, are all rejected by scripture including verses from Deuteronomy 6, Mathew 28, and John 1.[21]

For those unfamiliar with Christian doctrine, it states that God is one and that one holds three persons: The Father, Son, and Holy Spirit. Three persons in one nature or essence, a mystery. God is one and many at the same time, but not in the same sense. "He is one in the sense of his essence but many in the sense of his persons."[22] Further, *Christ is one person possessing both a divine and human nature at the same time.* He is unique. His death on the cross allowed his divine nature to overcome death—it gave Christ's death its meaning.

At one end of this category is Adoptionism. This heresy asserts Christ is two persons, or two sons: one of them God's son by nature (divine) and the other adopted (human). The man Christ was not a natural son but instead a good man. God is one person with one divine nature. The son was created by God but is not consubstantial with God the Father. Therefore, the son is not God. The man called Christ is human. Both distinct but within the same body.

At the other end of this spectrum is Modalism (Monarchianism). With this heresy, God is a cold, impersonal force. Jesus was a most pious man and born of a virgin. Christ came down during Jesus' baptism and appeared on the Earth as the son. This splits the Godhead, making Christ less than God. With both these heresies, Christ's sacrifice on the cross has no meaning as it was just the death of a good man.

Between these two is Arianism, a heresy influenced by Gnosticism. Christ is a second inferior godling (the Logos), one who created the world and in turn was created by God—because God alone is eternal. God is a cold, impersonal, almost alien force, one who put the universe into motion and then went away. Man limits God by saying He cannot have a son. As the son is not God, there is again no meaning to the cross and no redemption. Either God is all powerful or He is not. You cannot have it both ways. This heresy has similarities to Deism, and appealed to the elite ruling and military classes during the last centuries of Roman rule. Some modern Arianism examples include Jehovah's Witnesses and Unitarian Churches.

A fourth heresy has its roots in the writings of Plotinus, a third century philosopher. Plotinus was a pagan who despised Christianity. He posited all complex unities must have over them a simple unity. Within Plotinus' framework, a unity can only be either simple or complex. Simple unities can only be described in terms of what they are not. They are transcendent, beyond the reach of human understanding. Complex unities, on the other hand, can be described in terms of what they are. They are immanent, present in the world—we can know them.

According to Plotinus, the First Cause (what Christians would call God) must be a simple unity so far removed from human knowledge, so purely one, as to be absolutely inscrutable. There can be no being, person, essence, or nature. There can be no God as Christian doctrine proclaims. God is only a single, all-powerful will. This will is the cause of everything. Man is created a slave, and not free. Plotinus embraced the pagan thought that freedom is one's state when one is not coerced by another, because man's natural state is to be under another's coercion. So there can be no free will, only God's will. There is absolutely no room for the distinctions of a Godhead. As such, God cannot have a son, and man cannot have a relationship with God as there is no basis for one. A modern example is Islam.

The final heresy in this section is Donatism. This heresy occurred at the height of the Roman persecutions against Christians. Some North African Christians collaborated with the Romans. When the persecutions were over, they asked to be brought back into the body of Christian believers and were refused. The reason given was God's grace was insufficient, man limiting God's mercy and power. This heresy represents a failure by man to trust and obey God. Instead, man relies on himself. Its views represent a different form of elitism. You can see this heresy present today in the thoughts of people who hold organizations accountable for the actions of an individual.

<u>Christological</u>

Four heresies are mentioned in this category, all dealing with Christ's nature. The first two grew out of the Arian heresy mentioned above. We'll consider Nestorianism first. Nestorius was a bishop in Constantinople. He asserted that Mary was not the mother of God but only the man Jesus. There are two completely divisible natures within a single person: one divine and one human. He asserted that God could not have been born or died.

The second is Monophysitism, which began in Egypt as a response to Nestorianism. This heresy denied the incarnation, God becoming man. Christ had only one nature—divine—so He only appeared to suffer. As with the Trinitarian heresies, the denial of Christ's dual nature made moot his sacrifice on the cross. This heresy is present in many today who view themselves as spiritual, believing that Christ, being the Son of God and divine, must have only a divine nature.

Manichaeism is a third heresy and has significant gnostic underpinnings (see below). This heresy is a religious smorgasbord. It expressed the existence of two opposing forces, good and evil. Mani taught that Christ only seemed to have a body and only appeared to suffer. In reality the savior was the personification of cosmic light. He also taught salvation could be obtained only by knowledge. It was a form of elitism through possession of secret knowledge. The leaders within this sect were said to live very pure ascetic lives, but just about anything went for its worshippers. A modern example is the B'hai faith. Also of note, Augustine for a short time followed Manichaeism early in his adult life, later writing extensively against its beliefs and ideas.

This section's final heresy is Pelagianism. Unlike the other heresies mentioned, which largely came from the East, this one developed in Britain during the fourth century, and Augustine wrote extensively to refute its claims. His treatise on grace and free will used earlier was part of this body of literature.

Pelagius was a Christian monk who wanted to rescue Christianity from its crude thoughts. He denied original sin, saying that Adam simply made a bad choice. Further, man is capable of pulling himself up, a denial of God's grace needing to be present to do good. There is a strong connection between today's moral relativism and this heresy. There is also the notion that we are all inherently good; therefore, there are no differences between religions, and you must accept someone's beliefs whatever they may be. We can see its ideas in our culture today. These include thoughts such as *My sins don't affect anyone else*, *How can God hold me guilty for a sin I didn't commit*, and *Those are my views and you are intolerant if you don't accept them*. Modern examples include recent Disney media and today's interfaith movement.

Including Disney in this section may seem surprising, but their media reflect the cultural values just mentioned. In a 2014 interview, the songwriters of the Disney movie *Frozen* said the following about writing material for a princess musical today:[23]

GROSS: So, you know, "Frozen," there's like two princesses, and one of them becomes the queen. And I know like a lot of mothers, and probably fathers, too, are kind of disturbed when their children get into princess fantasies because it can be a very retro way of being female, of, you know, just being like, you know, so - everything's about being beautiful and being, you know, kissed and saved by the handsome prince and everything.

So Kristen, here you are writing a princess musical. Were there certain things that you knew you had to avoid?

ANDERSON-LOPEZ: Absolutely. In fact, if you have the deluxe CD, you will see my very strong strike across the bow at all princess myths, things in the form of a song called "We Know Better," ...

We both went through the '90s. We took the women's studies courses, and I knew I wouldn't be able to push my kids on the swing at the playground if I had written a movie where the girl wore the puffy dress and was saved not by anything active she did but by being beautiful enough to be kissed by a prince.

And a little later the following about working for Disney:

ANDERSON-LOPEZ: It's funny. One of the only places you have to draw the line at Disney is with religious things, the word God.

LOPEZ: Yeah. You just can't...

GROSS: You can't say the word God?

LOPEZ: There was even a - well, you can say it in Disney but you can't put it in the movie.

ANDERSON-LOPEZ: You can't put it in the movies.

The above ideas corrupt and belittle the virtues displayed by earlier female Disney characters like Snow White and Cinderella. Characters who were also being true to themselves. It's just these earlier character's had values rooted in the self-sacrifice and charity at the heart of Christian doctrine, and not the pagan self-interest prevalent today.

Gnosticism

Gnosticism is generally accepted today as having existed before Christianity. All heresies in this category involve having access to some additional secret knowledge required for salvation. It's an elitist idea because not all possess this secret knowledge and therefore those who do must be better than others—or else everyone would have this knowledge. The first two heresies concern God's revelations, and the last two more historical gnostic beliefs.

These first heresies are two of Christianity's oldest, dating to the second century. Marcionism is a dualistic belief that rejected Judaism. Its followers believed Jesus was not the son of the God of the Jews, but the son of another deity, the Good God. Marcion rejected the Old Testament and all other scripture except for some sections of Luke's gospel. He taught that God did not create the universe, but instead it was created by an inferior godling. Further, God wouldn't judge nor impose any morality upon man. It allows man to pick and choose what to accept from God—man elevating his thoughts above God's revelations. Modern examples include minimalists and many of today's liberal Catholic and Protestant scholars, such as the Jesus Seminar.

The second heresy is Montanism. It is the opposite of Marcionism. Montanus spoke in the person of God, saying "I am the Father, the Word, and the Paraclete (Holy Spirit)." He brought supposed-knowledge in the way of additional revelations from God. Montanus believed God sent him as the chooser and revealer, putting special wisdom into him. Modern examples of this heresy include Jehovah's Witnesses, The Church of Jesus Christ of Later-day Saints (Mormons), Christian Scientists, and Islam.

This section closes by looking at some general Gnostic beliefs and one final heresy with close connections to it. The underlying principle within this heresy was salvation through special knowledge alone, as already mentioned several times. It took the simple message of the Gospel and made it more complex by adding additional secret requirements. This aspect of special knowledge had great appeal to those who viewed themselves as the elite, an "I'm on the inside and you're not" mindset, the very opposite of the notions we should hold.

Within gnosticism, the universe was not created by God, but instead by an inferior jealous godling. There existed a struggle between good and evil, God's spirit and the matter created by the godling. The flesh was corrupt and the spirit good. Matter was to be rejected and the spirit embraced. Underlying this idea was a pagan philosophical and religious cynicism about creation. The gnostic special knowledge would allow the individual to overcome the godling and free us from corruption. This escape from the world would be made possible by a superhuman savior: Christ. Christ was not divine but simply a good moral teacher we are to learn from.

Arising from this heresy are many false gospels and texts—the secret knowledge. We know they are false as they were not written until the second or third century, one or two centuries after the four Gospels and other books of the New Testament were written. In addition, Christ within these gnostic gospels is not human, again a rejection of matter. Gnostic thought is not seen as being any different from Christian thought in today's culture. Go into many bookstores and you'll see gnostic books sitting alongside books on Christian doctrine, an indication of their acceptance within our society. Man is the object within all the gnostic heresies and not God. Modern examples include movies such as *The Da Vinci Code* and *The Matrix* series, Masonic organizations, and spaceship cults.

The final heresy is Docetism, which had strong gnostic connections. Within this sect, Christ was not human, only appearing to be a man. In fact, the root word for this heresy means *illusion*. Some went as far as to deny Christ's human nature altogether. He appeared without any birth from the virgin Mary, because matter was not created by God but an inferior godling.

Christ only appeared to be a man and to suffer and die. Someone else took Christ's place on the cross, and the witnesses were made to think it was Christ being crucified. This last idea also appears within the Basilidian heresy and Islam.

We've discussed most aspects of the model noted earlier, but one remains: the law. We are now ready for that discussion.

What About Law?

Law is where many works on natural rights begin, and we can look to law to gain some understanding of our rights. A legal definition of a right would go along the lines of *a proper claim or title to, or interest in, a thing*. But make no mistake, this definition is not the same as the one for rights at the very beginning of this chapter. A right *is* a proper moral claim, whereas law is concerned only *about* that claim. A law is about something; a right is the thing itself. Law is like a shadow. It follows from the claim granted by a right.

All law belongs to reason and is above all concerned with the plan of things for human happiness.[24] Not an individual happiness but a common one shared within a society. Every law is to be shaped for promoting the common good. This planning is the business of either the whole people or the person(s) responsible for their caretaking, because the power to coerce rests only with those having authority and not with individuals within a society.[25]

There are several different categories of law to consider. Thomas delineated several in his *Summa Theologicæ* that included eternal, divine, natural, and human. The categories are not clearly maintained within his writing, but they make some distinctions useful for our discussions. A century earlier Gratian just divided all ordinance into two categories, with all morality contained within divine ordinance and law in human ordinance. Further, all divine law per Gratian was natural law.[26]

While much of this section comes from Thomas' writings, the same concepts are expressed by many others including John Calvin, Ulrich Zwingli, Martin Bucer, Theodore Beza, Johannes Althusius, Edward Coke, John Milton, John Winthrop, John Cotton, Edmund Burke, and Jonathan Edwards, to name only a few.

Eternal Law

As to eternal law, "Law is nothing but a dictate or practical reason issued by a sovereign who governs a complete community. Granted that the world is ruled by divine Providence ... it is evident that the whole community of the universe is governed by God's mind. Therefore the ruling idea of things which exists in God as the effective sovereign of them all has the nature of law. Then since God's mind does not conceive in time, but has an eternal concept ... it follows that this law should be called eternal."[27]

Everyone has some knowledge of truth,[28] and insofar as all law shares in right reason, it is derived from eternal law.[29] All are subject to divine governance, so all are subject to eternal law.[30] Further all law is either divine or human.[31] Human law permits certain things, as it is unable to control all things. Divine law, on the other hand, directs things outside of human law, as a higher power directs a lower one.[32]

Divine Law

While human law is created by man, divine law is created by God. Every lawmaker intends to direct men toward his own end through the law, and the end to which God intends to direct men is God himself.[33] Divine law directs man toward becoming good, thus fulfilling our purpose.

Man needs divine law for the following reasons. First, human judgment is not always trustworthy. Second, one man cannot judge another man's heart, only his actions. Third, human law cannot punish everything or forbid all wrongdoing; it focuses on only the most egregious actions. Finally, and most importantly, the end God directs man to—becoming good—is happiness, the eternal peace mentioned earlier. That happiness is beyond man's own abilities to attain.[34] *God's law is necessary to direct man to God's end. Man is unable to do it alone.*

Natural Law

Natural law is man's sharing in eternal law, which doesn't change, using his natural reason to discern what is good and what is evil.[35] Good is to be sought, as it is our purpose, and evil to be avoided.[36] Man has a natural tendency toward good in creation. Remember man's creation was good. Evil is the absence of good, the result of man's choices when he turns away from good—God. Man has a natural bent toward things in accordance with his nature, and his rational reason is in accordance with good.[37]

Becoming good requires becoming righteous—that is, virtuous. Therefore, virtues are a matter of natural law.[38] The cardinal virtues of faith, hope, and charity (love) direct men toward God, while the moral virtues direct men in their interactions with each other. As good differs from evil, virtue differs from vice. They arise from different sources. Virtue "derives from man's desire for the changeless good; thus charity, the love of God, is described ... as the root of all virtue."[39] Vice, on the other hand, springs from the desire for transient goods, the material things of this world.

God's truth is changeless and the same for everyone. But some choose not to recognize that truth through the exercise of their free will.[40] However, this truth cannot be cancelled entirely from the human heart as grace is more powerful than nature.[41] As His truth is the same for everyone, so the principles of natural law are the same for everyone. However, there can in some instances be variance in the conclusions drawn from those principles.[42]

Natural law extends from eternal law, so its principles are unalterable by man. Natural law can only be added to by either divine or, as we'll see in a moment, human law.[43] As man uses his reason to determine natural law (discerning good from evil), the natural rights derived from that reason can be one of two kinds. The first are those set in nature. These are referred to as the laws of nature. The second are the laws of nature's God.

The first have to do with God's creation, and the second with His communications to man. This book is about the latter. There are many things man shares with the rest of creation, but it is easy to show that man uses his will to also violate the former. Two quick examples. In all of nature, relationships are formed between male and female for purposes of procreation. Where this doesn't happen is so rare it is an aberration. Only man actively believes it is okay to form and attempt to sustain same-sex relationships. Gender is determined by nature and not emotions. We can look to abortion for a second example. Within the animal kingdom, adults protect their offspring and will often sacrifice themselves for their young's safety. It is man alone who sometimes decides to kill his own young before they are born. Abortion's presence today is evidence that some are turned away from God, perhaps because they have never learned about Him.

Human Law

The first rule of reason is natural law. All human law, if just, flows from natural law.[44] The purpose of human law is to be useful to man. It is to be consistent with religion, fulfilling divine law. It is to agree with good discipline, supporting natural law. Finally, it is to further human welfare by supporting the common good.[45] It does this by incrementally bringing people to virtue. Human law can be divided between common and positive law. Common law relates to legal principles shared across political communities. Positive law relates to civil law. Both are referred to as human law within this work.

Not all human law is good. Two examples. First, property ownership is a matter of human law. At least three benefits arise from human law in this area. One, each individual takes more trouble to care for something that is their sole responsibility than that which is held in common by many. Two, human affairs are more efficiently organized if each one has their own responsibilities to discharge, rather than everyone being responsible for everything. Three, man lives together in greater peace when everyone is content with his work.[46] Property ownership promotes the common good.

Now a second example. Slavery is also a product of human law. It was supported into the early Middle Ages, and became prominent again during the Renaissance and Enlightenment periods. However, I doubt that anyone would seriously claim slavery promotes the common good. It does demonstrate that all human law must be viewed with some skepticism. We must ask of each human law, "Does it promote virtue and the common good?"

Man has an innate bent toward virtues, but education is required to form them. We are not born possessing virtue. We are given the ability to reason, but not knowledge. Knowledge must be acquired through an education in reason and faith, and then by our effort and practice virtues are formed. The premise for writing this book is education: that you may hear the truth and through your further efforts continue to grow. But not all choose to voluntarily acquire virtue. Some come to develop virtue through admonition and discipline, and others have a still more difficult time developing them and need to be held back by fear and force through law.[47]

All the preceding can be expressed in one simple idea. There can be no respect for persons if unequal people are not treated equally.[48] While we have an equal nature, which deserves equal treatment; we do not have the same skills, abilities, knowledge, or aptitudes. Some also choose to apply themselves more than others and experience relatively greater success. Human law is to complement natural law by looking to a community's safety. While human law allows for some dispensations, natural law allows for no dispensations from its principles.[49] Even the Prince [law-maker] is to be restrained by his own laws.[50]

Underlying this entire legal framework are several basic principles. First, that when a society is formed, there is a three-way covenant created between God, the ruler(s), and the people.[51] Second, all individuals submitting to God are each called to be prophets, priests, and kings[52]: prophets who are to educate others in the truth; priests who are to sacrifice for others; and, finally, kings who must first rule themselves using the law God has written on our hearts (natural law), while also sharing in the ruling and preservation of society. When man looks at the law alone, it is easy to bend it, then bend it a little more, and later still a little further. Eventually, when looking only to the law, man eventually loses sight of the original principle and then goes off-track.

Positive and Negative Rights

This work examines some rights we can derive from the laws of nature's God and therefore uses the Bible, God's communication to man, as its source. These rights can be classified as positive or negative. *A positive right within this work sets an expectation of performing a specific action, or receiving a certain benefit. The basis of a negative right is an expectation of refraining from something.* Both are grounded in morality. The first says you shall do something and the later that you will refrain from an action.

Natural rights come from God and are negative. Human rights are created by man and are generally positive ones. This should not be surprising. The ten commandments given by God to Moses (see pages 40 and 45-6) are things man is to refrain from doing. Take life as an example. We have a right to our life, but it is based on God's placing a limitation on man's actions—a negative right underlying the command not to kill. Although the natural rights outlined in this book are usually couched in positive terms, they represent negative rights.

The type of right matters because of the way it sets limits for acceptable behavior. *A positive right presents a limit on a specific action to be performed, and sometimes a requirement to perform such action.* A negative right presents a limit on action too. However, this limit is inherently different. *A negative right says you can choose from multiple actions up to where something specific is forbidden. You have freedom to choose across those actions with a negative right, but only the freedom to choose to perform a specific action with a positive right.* With God's law you must use your freedom responsibly. With human law one often gives up some, if not most, of their freedom in a specific area. In some respects, human law is simpler but not necessarily right.

But there is another reason why positive and negative rights matter. Negative rights seldom violate another person's rights, as all face the same limits. Positive rights, on the other hand, generally do violate another person's rights as it sets up conflicting priorities between the rights of individuals and/or groups. How can one have a positive right without violating another's negative right(s)? How can one have a positive right that in some circumstances does not take away from another persons or groups positive right(s)? There is a place for human rights, but the so called human rights being pushed by progressives today represent a false notion that is discussed further in Chapter 5.

Before closing, as noted earlier, a right is that which can be claimed on the basis of moral or just grounds. It is voluntary, leads to the creation of virtue, and results in actions performed out of love that fulfill divine law. Divine law can be summarized as simply loving God and our fellow man. There is one more word we need to define. We've already used it several times throughout this chapter: responsibility. *A responsibility is a duty or trust, something one is morally bound to do.* Underlying it all again is morality. Each right coming from God should have a corresponding moral responsibility for us. Within this work, the words *responsibility* and *duty* are used interchangeably as both represent the same idea.

We can go back to the earlier discussion of grace for this concept. God loves us. He's given us a gift: grace. If we act justly or righteously, shouldn't we return that love? This idea will be reflected in each of the natural rights discussed in the following three chapters. A right derives from love extended either by God (natural rights) or our fellow man (human rights). Accepting, or acting on, a right produces a responsibility, or duty if you like, of returning that love. Both are voluntary. Both are performed out of love. Both, if accepted, set expectations for behavior and the way we feel and view the other party.

The Remainder of This Book

We are now ready to develop a framework to consider natural rights. The framework will be at a high level, drawing quotations from the Bible for support. This approach is necessary as we each must derive natural law ourselves using our reason. While another can provide you with some guideposts, you must master the material by internalizing it for yourself.

This book's contents present the results of an analysis, the pieces, and how they fit together. These allow you to judge their worth. They have value in assisting you on your way, but they do not compare to the story of Christ contained in the Bible. My hope is that you will keep this work at hand and take occasion to review it and ponder on the contents as your understanding of that story grows. I'm not sure there is an end to this reflection. Internalizing natural law's principles will put your feet on the solid path leading to your fulfillment. Only you can do that, as your journey will likely not be exactly like anyone else's. For you are unique.

The next three chapters look at the areas of being, actions, and dominion. That will be followed by a chapter examining some features of today's culture, why we are off-track, and most importantly what we can do to change our direction.

Chapter 2

Being

This chapter lays out our foundational rights and duties used to examine our other natural rights and responsibilities. These rights relate to our being: who we are. Natural rights are dependent on God's nature and ours, and the relationship we are to have with each other. If we don't get those correct, then nothing else matters because our reason—without faith—leads us to a false conclusion. Therefore, we'll start with sections related to God's nature and ours, and then proceed into the rights and responsibilities noted in the diagram below arising from those relationships.

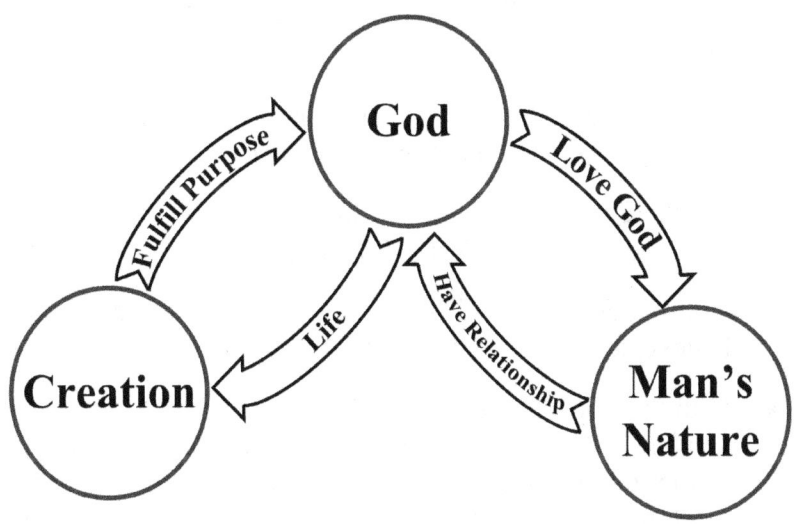

The rights and responsibilities noted above are very general. More detailed rights and responsibilities can be derived from these more general ones. As an example, in Chapter 4 we'll review some of the rights and responsibilities related to the dominion established in this chapter. One of those rights is for man to communicate with others. That communication can take place in a number of ways, including human speech, the printed word, telecommunications, and so on. The means, or channels by which man communicates, include what have been referred to historically as freedoms of speech and the press. More detailed rights derived from the same general one.

Who is God?

God is the creator of everything that has ever been created. As mentioned earlier, He is creation's governor. Other characteristics include being One, Eternal, and Triune—three persons in one nature. Verses related to each of these points are presented below. The list is not exhaustive, as that approach would end up incorporating a very large portion of the Bible. However, that is not necessary as we are interested in identifying some general principles that help us understand our natural rights. The cited verses are relevant and summarize many of the main points.

God Is One

- Hear, O Israel! The Lord is our God, the Lord is one! Deuteronomy 6:4 (also Ephesians 4:4-6)

- For there is one God, and one mediator also between God and men, the man Christ Jesus. 1 Timothy 2:5

- You believe that God is one. You do well; the demons also believe, and shudder. James 2:19

- I am the Lord, that is My name; / I will not give My glory to another, / Nor My praise to graven images. / Behold, the former things have come to pass, / Now I declare new things; / Before they spring forth I proclaim them to you. Isaiah 42:8-9

- Thus says the Lord, the King of Israel and his Redeemer, the Lord of hosts: / "I am the first and I am the last, / And there is no God besides Me. / Who is like Me? Let him proclaim and declare it; / Yes, let him recount it to Me in order, / From the time that I established the ancient nation. / And let them declare to them the things that are coming / And the events that are going to take place. / Do not tremble and do not be afraid; / Have I not long since announced it to you and declared it? / And you are My witnesses. / Is there any God besides Me, / Or is there any other Rock? / I know of none." Isaiah 44:6-8

- Then Moses said to God, "Behold, I am going to the sons of Israel, and I will say to them, 'The God of your fathers has sent me to you.' Now they may say to me, 'What is His name?' What shall I say to them?" God said to Moses, "I AM WHO I AM"; and He said, "Thus you shall say to the sons of Israel, 'I AM has sent me to you.'" Exodus 3:13-4

Eternal

- In the beginning was the Word, and the Word was with God, and the Word was God. He was with God in the beginning. John 1:1-2

- "I am the Alpha and the Omega," says the Lord God, "who is and who was and who is to come, the Almighty." Revelations 1:8 (also Revelations. 22:13)

- "You are My witnesses," declares the Lord, / "And My servant whom I have chosen, / So that you may know and believe Me / And understand that I am He. / Before Me there was no God formed, / And there will be none after Me. / I, even I, am the Lord, / And there is no savior besides Me." Isaiah 43:10-1

Creator

- In the beginning God created the heavens and the earth. Genesis 1:1 (also Isaiah 45:11-3)

- Through him [the Word] all things were made; without him nothing was made that has been made. In him was life, and that life was the light of all mankind. John 1:3-4

Triune

- And Jesus came up and spoke to them, saying, "All authority has been given to Me in heaven and on earth. Go therefore and make disciples of all the nations, baptizing them in the name of the Father and the Son and the Holy Spirit, teaching them to observe all that I commanded you; and lo, I am with you always, even to the end of the age." Matthew 28:18-20

The next passages examine some of the distinctions and similarities between the three persons mentioned in the previous passage. Three persons within one nature is a mystery to us as human beings. But God knows; we do not. Denial of what He has told us about Himself is man placing limitations on God. For more regarding that line of thought, see the Heresies section in the previous chapter.

Father

As Father, God is creation's king, all-powerful and all-knowing. There is nothing which He cannot do, nor anything He does not see. As He is eternal, He stands outside of time and does not change. He is also love and good, the source of all morality. We are to know Him through his creation, revelations, and the spirit He put within each one of us.

- But the Lord is the true God; / He is the living God and the everlasting King. / At His wrath the earth quakes, / And the nations cannot endure His indignation. Jeremiah 10:10 (also Deuteronomy 4:39)

- Looking at them, Jesus said, "With people it is impossible, but not with God; for all things are possible with God." Mark 10:27

- "Am I a God who is near," declares the Lord, / "And not a God far off?" / "Can a man hide himself in hiding places / So I do not see him?" declares the Lord. / "Do I not fill the heavens and the earth?" declares the Lord. Jeremiah 23:23-4

- Every good thing given and every perfect gift is from above, coming down from the Father of lights, with whom there is no variation or shifting shadow. James 1:17-8 (see also 1 John 1:5)

- Beloved, let us love one another, for love is from God; and everyone who loves is born of God and knows God. The one who does not love does not know God, for God is love. By this the love of God was manifested in us, that God has sent His only begotten Son into the world so that we might live through Him. In this is love, not that we loved God, but that He loved us and sent His Son to be the propitiation for our sins. 1 John 4:7-10 (also 1 Corinthians 8:3)

- To you it was shown that you might know that the Lord, He is God; there is no other besides Him. Out of the heavens He let you hear His voice to discipline you; and on earth He let you see His great fire, and you heard His words from the midst of the fire. Because He loved your fathers, therefore He chose their descendants after them. Deuteronomy 4:35-7

Son

The Son shares many of the same attributes with the Father. He, too, is One, Eternal, all-knowing, and changeless. Yet He is the image of the Father; the Son is also distinct. He is the way to God, creator, life, heir, and judge. Through the Son's death we received salvation, and His birth was foretold over seven hundred years before it occurred by the prophet Isaiah and others.

- Jesus said to them, "Truly, truly, I say to you, before Abraham was born, I am." John 8:58

- Jesus Christ is the same yesterday and today and forever. Hebrews 13:8 (also Isaiah 40:8)

- Jesus said to him, "I am the way, and the truth, and the life; no one comes to the Father but through Me." John 14:6

- And Jesus said to him, "Why do you call Me good? No one is good except God alone." Mark 10:18

- While he was speaking, a cloud appeared and covered them, and they were afraid as they entered the cloud. A voice came from the cloud, saying, "This is my Son, whom I have chosen; listen to him." Luke 9:34-5 (also Matthew 17:5, Mark 9:7)

- [I]n these last days has spoken to us in His Son, whom He appointed heir of all things, through whom also He made the world. And He is the radiance of His glory and the exact representation of His nature, and upholds all things by the word of His power. When He had made purification of sins, He sat down at the right hand of the Majesty on high. Hebrew 1:2-3 (also John 5:19-20)

- Therefore, since the children share in flesh and blood, He Himself [Christ] likewise also partook of the same, that through death He might render powerless him who had the power of death, that is, the devil, and might free those who through fear of death were subject to slavery all their lives. For assuredly He does not give help to angels, but He gives help to the descendants of Abraham. Therefore, He had to be made like His brethren in all things, so that He might become a merciful and faithful high priest in things pertaining to God, to make propitiation for the sins of the people. For since He Himself was tempted in that which He has suffered, He is able to come to the aid of those who are tempted. Hebrews 2:14-8

- For as the Father has life in himself, so he has granted the Son also to have life in himself. And he has given him authority to judge because he is the Son of Man. John 5:26-7 (also 5:22)

- For a child will be born to us, a son will be given to us; / And the government will rest on His shoulders; / And His name will be called Wonderful Counselor, Mighty God, / Eternal Father, Prince of Peace. / There will be no end to the increase of His government or of peace, / On the throne of David and over his kingdom, / To establish it and to uphold it with justice and righteousness / From then on and forevermore. / The zeal of the Lord of hosts will accomplish this. Isaiah 9:6-7 (also Romans 1:2-6)

Holy Spirit

The Holy Spirit is our helper, our counselor through whom we receive the spirit of truth and life.

- I will ask the Father, and He will give you another Helper, that He may be with you forever; that is the Spirit of truth, whom the world cannot receive, because it does not see Him or know Him, but you know Him because He abides with you and will be in you. John 14:16-7

- "When the Helper comes, whom I will send to you from the Father, that is the Spirit of truth who proceeds from the Father, He will testify about Me, and you will testify also, because you have been with Me from the beginning." John 15:26-7

- However, you are not in the flesh but in the Spirit, if indeed the Spirit of God dwells in you. But if anyone does not have the Spirit of Christ, he does not belong to Him. If Christ is in you, though the body is dead because of sin, yet the spirit is alive because of righteousness. But if the Spirit of Him who raised Jesus from the dead dwells in you, He who raised Christ Jesus from the dead will also give life to your mortal bodies through His Spirit who dwells in you. Romans 8:9-11

Summary

So who is God? He is One and Eternal. He is good and love, and therefore the source of morality. He will judge man in the last days, but also offers us the means of salvation—if we choose to partake of it. He intends for us to have a relationship with Him through the Son and Holy Spirit. He created everything that was ever created. As we are His creation, He must love us. Otherwise He wouldn't have created us. Why would someone who is good create what they did not love? We'll look at some passages related to life itself next before proceeding to look at man's nature.

Creation

As mentioned again in the last section, God is the creator of all things, including all life. Man was created differently from the rest of creation, as God breathed His spirit into him. All man was created from one man. All living things were created male and female to perpetuate life. Some verses regarding life in general are presented below.

- God saw all that He had made, and behold, it was very good. And there was evening and there was morning, the sixth day. Genesis 1:31

- Then the Lord God formed man of dust from the ground, and breathed into his nostrils the breath of life; and man became a living being. Genesis 2:7

- It is the Spirit who gives life; the flesh profits nothing; the words that I have spoken to you are spirit and are life. John 6:63

- Thus the heavens and the earth were completed, and all their hosts. By the seventh day God completed His work which He had done, and He rested on the seventh day from all His work which He had done. Genesis 2:1-2

- The man gave names to all the cattle, and to the birds of the sky, and to every beast of the field, but for Adam there was not found a helper suitable for him. So the Lord God caused a deep sleep to fall upon the man, and he slept; then He took one of his ribs and closed up the flesh at that place. The Lord God fashioned into a woman the rib which He had taken from the man, and brought her to the man. Genesis 2:20-2

- But from the beginning of creation, God made them male and female. For this reason a man shall leave his father and mother, and the two shall become one flesh; so they are no longer two, but one flesh. What therefore God has joined together, let no man separate. Mark 10:6-9 (also Genesis 2:24, Matthew 19:5-6, and Ephesians 5:31)

Man received the breath of God at his creation, God's spirit. Man was also given a unique position within creation. While man is still a part of creation, creation was made for man's use. Man was given dominion over it, as we'll see next.

Who is Man?

As just noted, man was created differently from the rest of creation. Some of the implications from that difference are outlined in this section. We were created for a specific purpose, to do good. As a part of God's creation, man belongs to God, although man also has the free will to choose whether he will accept God as his sovereign. We are finite, equal in nature, all heirs to the same inheritance, created in freedom, and called to be a single people. We are also fallen through sin, but redeemed by His grace.

Created to Do Good

- For we are His workmanship, created in Christ Jesus for good works, which God prepared beforehand so that we would walk in them. Ephesians 2:10

- With good will render service, as to the Lord, and not to men, knowing that whatever good thing each one does, this he will receive back from the Lord, whether slave or free. Ephesians 6:7-8

- Then God said, "Let Us make man in Our image, according to Our likeness; and let them rule over the fish of the sea and over the birds of the sky and over the cattle and over all the earth, and over every creeping thing that creeps on the earth." God created man in His own image, in the image of God He created him; male and female He created them. God blessed them; and God said to them, "Be fruitful and multiply, and fill the earth, and subdue it; and rule over the fish of the sea and over the birds of the sky and over every living thing that moves on the earth." Genesis 1:26-8

We Belong to God

- But now, thus says the Lord, your Creator, O Jacob, / And He who formed you, O Israel, / "Do not fear, for I have redeemed you; / I have called you by name; you are Mine! / When you pass through the waters, I will be with you; / And through the rivers, they will not overflow you. / When you walk through the fire, you will not be scorched, / Nor will the flame burn you. / For I am the Lord your God, / The Holy One of Israel, your Savior; / I have given Egypt as your ransom, / Cush and Seba in your place." Isaiah 43:1-3

- You will say to me then, "Why does He still find fault? For who resists His will?" On the contrary, who are you, O man, who answers back to God? The thing molded will not say to the molder, "Why did you make me like this," will it? Or does not the potter have a right over the clay, to make from the same lump one vessel for honorable use and another for common use? Romans 9:19-21 (also Isaiah 29:15-6, 41:25-7, 45:9-10, 64:8, and Jeremiah 18:1-10)

- If some of the branches have been broken off, and you, though a wild olive shoot, have been grafted in among the others and now share in the nourishing sap from the olive root, do not consider yourself to be superior to those other branches. If you do, consider this: You do not support the root, but the root supports you. You will say then, "Branches were broken off so that I could be grafted in." Granted. But they were broken off because of unbelief, and you stand by faith. Do not be arrogant, but tremble. For if God did not spare the natural branches, he will not spare you either. Romans 11:17-9 (also John 15:1-7)

Man is Finite with an Uncertain Future

- For I have taken all this to my heart and explain it that righteous men, wise men, and their deeds are in the hand of God. Man does not know whether it will be love or hatred; anything awaits him. It is the same for all. There is one fate for the righteous and for the wicked; for the good, for the clean and for the unclean; for the man who offers a sacrifice and for the one who does not sacrifice. As the good man is, so is the sinner; as the swearer is, so is the one who is afraid to swear. Ecclesiastes 9:1-2 (also Ecclesiastes 2:16 and 9:11-2)

- Do you not know that when you present yourselves to someone as slaves for obedience, you are slaves of the one whom you obey, either of sin resulting in death, or of obedience resulting in righteousness? Romans 6:16 (also Ezekiel 18:31-2)

- "Present your case," the Lord says. / "Bring forward your strong arguments," / The King of Jacob says. / "Let them bring forth and declare to us what is going to take place; / As for the former events, declare what they were, / That we may consider them and know their outcome. / Or announce to us what is coming; / Declare the things that are going to come afterward, / That we may know that you are gods; / Indeed, do good or evil, that we may anxiously look about us and fear together. / Behold, you are of no account, / And your work amounts to nothing; / He who chooses you is an abomination." Isaiah 41:21-4

By Nature We Are All Equal and Heirs

- Do we not all have one father? Has not one God created us? Why do we deal treacherously each against his brother so as to profane the covenant of our fathers? Malachi 2:10

- As for the assembly, there shall be one statute for you and for the alien who sojourns with you, a perpetual statute throughout your generations; as you are, so shall the alien be before the Lord. There is to be one law and one ordinance for you and for the alien who sojourns with you. Numbers 15:15-6 (also Leviticus 24:22 and 19:33-4)

- For there is no distinction between Jew and Greek; for the same Lord is Lord of all, abounding in riches for all who call on Him; for "Whoever will call on the name of the Lord will be saved." Romans 10:12-3 (also Galatians 5:6)

- For you are all sons of God through faith in Christ Jesus. For all of you who were baptized into Christ have clothed yourselves with Christ. There is neither Jew nor Greek, there is neither slave nor free man, there is neither male nor female; for you are all one in Christ Jesus. And if you belong to Christ, then you are Abraham's descendants, heirs according to promise. Galatians 3:26-9

No Longer Slaves, But His Children

- No longer do I call you slaves, for the slave does not know what his master is doing; but I have called you friends, for all things that I have heard from My Father I have made known to you. You did not choose Me but I chose you, and appointed you that you would go and bear fruit, and that your fruit would remain, so that whatever you ask of the Father in My name He may give to you. This I command you, that you love one another. John 15:15-7

- It was for freedom that Christ set us free; therefore keep standing firm and do not be subject again to a yoke of slavery. Galatians 5:1

- For you were called to freedom, brethren; only do not turn your freedom into an opportunity for the flesh, but through love serve one another. For the whole Law is fulfilled in one word, in the statement, "You shall love your neighbor as yourself." Galatians 5:13-4

Called to Be a People

- For even as the body is one and yet has many members, and all the members of the body, though they are many, are one body, so also is Christ. For by one Spirit we were all baptized into one body, whether Jews or Greeks, whether slaves or free, and we were all made to drink of one Spirit. 1 Corinthians 12:12-4

- But you are a chosen people, a royal priesthood, a holy nation, God's special possession, that you may declare the praises of him who called you out of darkness into his wonderful light. Once you were not a people, but now you are the people of God; once you had not received mercy, but now you have received mercy. 1 Peter 2:9-10 (also Hosea 1:10)

Fallen Through Sin

- Then Noah built an altar to the Lord, and took of every clean animal and of every clean bird and offered burnt offerings on the altar. The Lord smelled the soothing aroma; and the Lord said to Himself, "I will never again curse the ground on account of man, for the intent of man's heart is evil from his youth; and I will never again destroy every living thing, as I have done. While the earth remains, seedtime and harvest, and cold and heat, and summer and winter, and day and night shall not cease." Genesis 8:20-2

- If we say that we have no sin, we are deceiving ourselves and the truth is not in us. If we confess our sins, He is faithful and righteous to forgive us our sins and to cleanse us from all unrighteousness. If we say that we have not sinned, we make Him a liar and His word is not in us. 1 John 1:8-10

- What then? Are we better than they? Not at all; for we have already charged that both Jews and Greeks are all under sin; as it is written, "There is none righteous, not even one; There is none who understands, there is none who seeks for God; all have turned aside, together they have become useless; there is none who does good, there is not even one." Romans 3:9-12 (also Psalm 14:3)

But Redeemed By Grace

- [F]or you have been born again not of seed which is perishable but imperishable, that is, through the living and enduring word of God. 1 Peter 1:23

- For the promise is for you and your children and for all who are far off, as many as the Lord our God will call to Himself. Acts 2:39 (also Isaiah 53:6)

- Do not say in your heart when the Lord your God has driven them out before you, "Because of my righteousness the Lord has brought me in to possess this land," but it is because of the wickedness of these nations that the Lord is dispossessing them before you. It is not for your righteousness or for the uprightness of your heart that you are going to possess their land, but it is because of the wickedness of these nations that the Lord your God is driving them out before you, in order to confirm the oath which the Lord swore to your fathers, to Abraham, Isaac and Jacob. Deuteronomy 9:4-5

- And He did so to make known the riches of His glory upon vessels of mercy, which He prepared beforehand for glory, even us, whom He also called, not from among Jews only, but also from among Gentiles. Romans 9:23-4

Summary

Like the rest of creation, man's nature is finite and not eternal. Through receiving God's image, man was given reason and freedom (Chapter 3). We have a specific purpose and the ability to choose whether we pursue that purpose or not. Man was also given dominion over the rest of creation (Chapter 4), but man still belongs to his creator. Man sometimes chooses wrong. As God is good, He must be just. Therefore, when man chooses wrong, he deserves punishment. However, that punishment has been taken by Christ on our behalf, an act of love—grace.

Man was given life and God's image, an inward image—reason and spirit—in order to do good. To love. This love is to extend to both God and our fellow man. This is the basis for our first two natural rights. These are the right to love God and live our lives, the right not to have that life taken from us. As noted earlier, although natural rights are sometimes worded as positive, they are actually negative rights.

Our Right to Love God ...

Again, through His act of creation, God is governor. Governance requires communication between the one who governs and those governed. We must know Him and what He asks of us. Growing in understanding requires applying our God-given reason to God's revelations (His word), His creation, and His image given to man. So what does God require from us? Simply to know Him, respect His authority, love Him, and choose to obey Him. These points are laid out below.

It is up to us to choose whether to accept this right. Saying yes places us in a covenant relationship with God, creating a duty for us to maintain a relationship with Him. This duty arises for our own good, out of love, as outlined in one of the passages below. This requires voluntarily becoming His disciple through knowing the Son and coming to Him as a child, in innocence, humility, and trust—in short, in virtue. Points related to this responsibility follow in the next section.

What We are to Know

- You shall be My people, / And I will be your God. Jeremiah 30:22

- Now, Israel, what does the Lord your God require from you, but to fear the Lord your God, to walk in all His ways and love Him, and to serve the Lord your God with all your heart and with all your soul, and to keep the Lord's commandments and His statutes which I am commanding you today for your good? Behold, to the Lord your God belong heaven and the highest heavens, the earth and all that is in it. Yet on your fathers did the Lord set His affection to love them, and He chose their descendants after them, even you above all peoples, as it is this day. Deuteronomy 10:12-5

- You shall love the Lord your God with all your heart and with all your soul and with all your might. Deuteronomy 6:5 (also Matthew 22:37, Mark 12:30, and Luke 10:27)

- Know therefore that the Lord your God, He is God, the faithful God, who keeps His covenant and His lovingkindness to a thousandth generation with those who love Him and keep His commandments. Deuteronomy 7:9

- Do not think that I [Jesus] have come to abolish the Law or the Prophets; I have not come to abolish them but to fulfill them. Matthew 5:17

- Then the Lord spoke to you from the midst of the fire; you heard the sound of words, but you saw no form—only a voice. So He declared to you His covenant which He commanded you to perform, that is, the Ten Commandments; and He wrote them on two tablets of stone. Deuteronomy 4:12-3 (also Genesis 17:1-8)

- The blood of goats and bulls and the ashes of a heifer sprinkled on those who are ceremonially unclean sanctify them so that they are outwardly clean. How much more, then, will the blood of Christ, who through the eternal Spirit offered himself unblemished to God, cleanse our consciences from acts that lead to death, so that we may serve the living God! For this reason Christ is the mediator of a new covenant, that those who are called may receive the promised eternal inheritance—now that he has died as a ransom to set them free from the sins committed under the first covenant. Hebrews 9:13-5

What We are to Do

- I am the Lord your God, who brought you out of the land of Egypt, out of the house of slavery.
    - You shall have no other gods before Me. (also Deuteronomy 6:14-5, Psalm 115:2-8, and 135:15-8)
    - You shall not make for yourself an idol, or any likeness of what is in heaven above or on the earth beneath or in the water under the earth. You shall not worship them or serve them; for I, the Lord your God, am a jealous God, visiting the iniquity of the fathers on the children, on the third and the fourth generations of those who hate Me, but showing lovingkindness to thousands, to those who love Me and keep My commandments.
    - You shall not take the name of the Lord your God in vain, for the Lord will not leave him unpunished who takes His name in vain.
    - Remember the sabbath day, to keep it holy. Six days you shall labor and do all your work, but the seventh day is a sabbath of the Lord your God; in it you shall not do any work, you or your son or your daughter, your male or your female servant or your cattle or your sojourner who stays with you. For in six days the Lord made the heavens and the earth, the sea and all that is in them, and rested on the seventh day; therefore the Lord blessed the sabbath day and made it holy. Exodus 20:2-11

Summary

We are to put God first, then everything else follows. Man strays when he finds idols to put in God's rightful place and turns away from His commands. Idols can be just about anything, from material things (such as cars, houses, drugs, alcohol, or money) to intangible items (such as power or a focus on oneself).

... And Duty to Have a Relationship with Him

God is love, and love can only be experienced. Therefore, in order to love God, we must do things to form a relationship—to experience His love. This goes back to the discussion of grace in the previous chapter. God loves us. He has given us the gift of mercy despite our disobedience at times. He desires we return the love He's shown us. We are to know God and do what He requires by becoming Christ's disciples and learning from the Son's example—in conjunction with the Holy Spirit. He has told us what we need to do to know Him.

Know the Son

- If you had known Me, you would have known My Father also; from now on you know Him, and have seen Him. John 14:7

- The glory which You have given Me I have given to them, that they may be one, just as We are one; I in them and You in Me, that they may be perfected in unity, so that the world may know that You sent Me, and loved them, even as You have loved Me. John 17:22-3

Become His Disciple

- Then he said to them all: "Whoever wants to be my disciple must deny themselves and take up their cross daily and follow me. For whoever wants to save their life will lose it, but whoever loses their life for me will save it. What good is it for someone to gain the whole world, and yet lose or forfeit their very self? Whoever is ashamed of me and my words, the Son of Man will be ashamed of them when he comes in his glory and in the glory of the Father and of the holy angels. Truly I tell you, some who are standing here will not taste death before they see the kingdom of God." Luke 9:23-7

- "If anyone comes to me and does not hate father and mother, wife and children, brothers and sisters—yes, even their own life—such a person cannot be my disciple. And whoever does not carry their cross and follow me cannot be my disciple." Luke 14:26-7

Come to Him as a Child In Service

- Then he said to them, "Whoever welcomes this little child in my name welcomes me; and whoever welcomes me welcomes the one who sent me. For it is the one who is least among you all who is the greatest." Luke 9:48

- And He called a child to Himself and set him before them, and said, "Truly I say to you, unless you are converted and become like children, you will not enter the kingdom of heaven. Whoever then humbles himself as this child, he is the greatest in the kingdom of heaven. And whoever receives one such child in My name receives Me; but whoever causes one of these little ones who believe in Me to stumble, it would be better for him to have a heavy millstone hung around his neck, and to be drowned in the depth of the sea. Matthew 18:2-6 (also Luke 18:15-7 and Mark 10:13-6)

- The Spirit Himself testifies with our spirit that we are children of God, and if children, heirs also, heirs of God and fellow heirs with Christ, if indeed we suffer with Him so that we may also be glorified with Him. Romans 8:16-7

Our Right to Life ...

As all life comes from God, creation's ruler, all life is sacred. It is God's first gift to us. It does not matter whether that life is inside or outside of the womb,[1] because each human being has a right to those things necessary to support life. These include the basics such as food, water, clothing, and shelter, which are often combined under the heading of property. But this right is not just limited to the physical things required for life, but also those intangibles allowing one to successfully live it and fulfill our purpose. These intangibles include behaviors and attitudes such as honor, truthfulness, respect, protection, and contentment with what you have.

Accepting this right creates a duty for us to try and fulfill our purpose as best we can. Becoming virtuous requires us to focus on the eternal, serving others out of love and being content with our lot while also trying to become the best individuals we can be. We will know how well we do by the fruit that comes from our actions. We will be judged not on our success but upon our heart and effort to try and do the right things.

What We are to Know

- [Y]et for us there is but one God, the Father, from whom are all things and we exist for Him; and one Lord, Jesus Christ, by whom are all things, and we exist through Him. 1 Corinthians 8:6

1. <u>God Does not Need Us, Man Needs Him</u>

- Do you not know that you are a temple of God and that the Spirit of God dwells in you? If any man destroys the temple of God, God will destroy him, for the temple of God is holy, and that is what you are. 1 Corinthians 3:16-7

- The God who made the world and all things in it, since He is Lord of heaven and earth, does not dwell in temples made with hands; nor is He served by human hands, as though He needed anything, since He Himself gives to all people life and breath and all things; and He made from one man every nation of mankind to live on all the face of the earth, having determined their appointed times and the boundaries of their habitation. Acts 17:24-6

- [A]nd He made from one man every nation of mankind to live on all the face of the earth, having determined their appointed times and the boundaries of their habitation, that they would seek God, if perhaps they might grope for Him and find Him, though He is not far from each one of us; for in Him we live and move and exist, as even some of your own poets have said, "For we also are His children." Acts 17:26-8

- He humbled you and let you be hungry, and fed you with manna which you did not know, nor did your fathers know, that He might make you understand that man does not live by bread alone, but man lives by everything that proceeds out of the mouth of the Lord. Deuteronomy 8:3

2. <u>Man's Dominion Includes Preserving Life</u>

- Every moving thing that is alive shall be food for you; I give all to you, as I gave the green plant. Only you shall not eat flesh with its life, that is, its blood. Surely I will require your lifeblood; from every beast I will require it. And from every man, from every man's brother I will require the life of man. "Whoever sheds man's blood, by man his blood shall be shed, for in the image of God He made man." Genesis 9:3-6

- "I have made the earth, the men and the beasts which are on the face of the earth by My great power and by My outstretched arm, and I will give it to the one who is pleasing in My sight." Jeremiah 27: 5

What We are to Do

- Honor your father and your mother, that your days may be prolonged in the land which the Lord your God gives you.

- You shall not murder.

- You shall not commit adultery.

- You shall not steal.

- You shall not bear false witness against your neighbor.

- You shall not covet your neighbor's house; you shall not covet your neighbor's wife or his male servant or his female servant or his ox or his donkey or anything that belongs to your neighbor. Exodus 20:12-7

- You shall not hate your fellow countryman in your heart; you may surely reprove your neighbor, but shall not incur sin because of him. You shall not take vengeance, nor bear any grudge against the sons of your people, but you shall love your neighbor as yourself; I am the Lord. Leviticus 19:17-8 (also Matthew 19:19, 22:39; Mark 12:31; Luke 10:27; Romans 13:9)

- When a stranger resides with you in your land, you shall not do him wrong. The stranger who resides with you shall be to you as the native among you, and you shall love him as yourself, for you were aliens in the land of Egypt; I am the Lord your God. Leviticus 19:33-4

- I know that there is nothing better for them than to rejoice and to do good in one's lifetime; moreover, that every man who eats and drinks sees good in all his labor—it is the gift of God. I know that everything God does will remain forever; there is nothing to add to it and there is nothing to take from it, for God has so worked that men should fear Him. That which is has been already and that which will be has already been, for God seeks what has passed by. Ecclesiastes 3:12-5

- But we urge you, brethren, to excel still more, and to make it your ambition to lead a quiet life and attend to your own business and work with your hands, just as we commanded you. 1 Thessalonians 4:10-1 (also 2 Thessalonians 3:7-11)

Summary

We have the right to live our lives, as long as we do not take another's life or the things needed to sustain another's life. In short, our actions are not to infringe on someone else's right to live their life as well through depriving them of either the physical or intangible things enabling them to live successfully. This effort requires stewardship and charity towards others, which are the subjects for additional rights in the following chapters. The rules for man's living with others basically comes down to honor, respect, and honesty. Honor for those in authority. Respect for others' possessions, and honesty in our relationships. All are subject to these same requirements as we share the same nature. We'll close this chapter looking at the responsibility from accepting the right to life.

... And Obligation to Fulfill Our Purpose

Each life is a gift from God; we therefore have an obligation to make the most of that gift—by fulfilling our purpose as best we can. Our purpose is fulfilled through knowing and doing, based upon what our governor (God) proclaims and directs.

We Are to Both Know and Do

- "Therefore everyone who hears these words of Mine and acts on them, may be compared to a wise man who built his house on the rock. And the rain fell, and the floods came, and the winds blew and slammed against that house; and yet it did not fall, for it had been founded on the rock. Everyone who hears these words of Mine and does not act on them, will be like a foolish man who built his house on the sand. The rain fell, and the floods came, and the winds blew and slammed against that house; and it fell—and great was its fall." Matthew 7:24-7 (also Luke 6:46-9)

What We Are to Know

1. <u>Look to the Eternal and Not the Temporary</u>

- In all your ways acknowledge Him, / And He will make your paths straight. / Do not be wise in your own eyes; / Fear the Lord and turn away from evil. / It will be healing to your body / And refreshment to your bones. / Honor the Lord from your wealth / And from the first of all your produce. Proverbs 3:6-9 (also Proverbs 1:15-9)

- But the one who joins himself to the Lord is one spirit with Him. Flee immorality. Every other sin that a man commits is outside the body, but the immoral man sins against his own body. Or do you not know that your body is a temple of the Holy Spirit who is in you, whom you have from God, and that you are not your own? For you have been bought with a price: therefore glorify God in your body. 1 Corinthians 6:17-20

- But have nothing to do with worldly fables fit only for old women. On the other hand, discipline yourself for the purpose of godliness; for bodily discipline is only of little profit, but godliness is profitable for all things, since it holds promise for the present life and also for the life to come. 1 Timothy 4:7-8

- But store up for yourselves treasures in heaven, where neither moth nor rust destroys, and where thieves do not break in or steal; for where your treasure is, there your heart will be also. Matthew 6:20-1

2. God Will Test Us

- My son, do not reject the discipline of the Lord / Or loathe His reproof, / For whom the Lord loves He reproves, / Even as a father corrects the son in whom he delights. Proverbs 3:11-2

- It is for discipline that you endure; God deals with you as with sons; for what son is there whom his father does not discipline? But if you are without discipline, of which all have become partakers, then you are illegitimate children and not sons. Furthermore, we had earthly fathers to discipline us, and we respected them; shall we not much rather be subject to the Father of spirits, and live? For they disciplined us for a short time as seemed best to them, but He disciplines us for our good, so that we may share His holiness. Hebrews 12:7-10

3. Be Content

- But godliness actually is a means of great gain when accompanied by contentment. For we have brought nothing into the world, so we cannot take anything out of it either. If we have food and covering, with these we shall be content. But those who want to get rich fall into temptation and a snare and many foolish and harmful desires which plunge men into ruin and destruction. For the love of money is a root of all sorts of evil, and some by longing for it have wandered away from the faith and pierced themselves with many griefs. 1 Timothy 6:6-10

4. Produce Good Fruit By Serving Others

- Wives, be subject to your husbands, as is fitting in the Lord. Husbands, love your wives and do not be embittered against them. Children, be obedient to your parents in all things, for this is well-pleasing to the Lord. Fathers, do not exasperate your children, so that they will not lose heart. Colossians 2:18-21 (also Colossians 3:20-1)

- If anyone thinks himself to be religious, and yet does not bridle his tongue but deceives his own heart, this man's religion is worthless. Pure and undefiled religion in the sight of our God and Father is this: to visit orphans and widows in their distress, and to keep oneself unstained by the world. James 1:26-7

- For there is no good tree which produces bad fruit, nor, on the other hand, a bad tree which produces good fruit. For each tree is known by its own fruit. For men do not gather figs from thorns, nor do they pick grapes from a briar bush. The good man out of the good treasure of his heart brings forth what is good; and the evil man out of the evil treasure brings forth what is evil; for his mouth speaks from that which fills his heart. Luke 6:43-5 (also Micah 7:11-3, Matthew 7:16-20 and 12:33-5)

5. Become Righteous (Virtuous)

- Or do you not know that the unrighteous will not inherit the kingdom of God? Do not be deceived; neither fornicators, nor

- idolaters, nor adulterers, nor effeminate, nor homosexuals, nor thieves, nor the covetous, nor drunkards, nor revilers, nor swindlers, will inherit the kingdom of God. Such were some of you; but you were washed, but you were sanctified, but you were justified in the name of the Lord Jesus Christ and in the Spirit of our God. 1 Corinthians 6:9-11 (also Ezekiel 18:5-9 and 1 Corinthians 6:13-6)

- So, as those who have been chosen of God, holy and beloved, put on a heart of compassion, kindness, humility, gentleness and patience; bearing with one another, and forgiving each other, whoever has a complaint against anyone; just as the Lord forgave you, so also should you. Beyond all these things put on love, which is the perfect bond of unity. Let the peace of Christ rule in your hearts, to which indeed you were called in one body; and be thankful. Let the word of Christ richly dwell within you, with all wisdom teaching and admonishing one another with psalms and hymns and spiritual songs, singing with thankfulness in your hearts to God. Whatever you do in word or deed, do all in the name of the Lord Jesus, giving thanks through Him to God the Father. Colossians 3:12-7

6. <u>Leaders Held to Higher Standards</u>

- It is a trustworthy statement: if any man aspires to the office of overseer, it is a fine work he desires to do. An overseer, then, must be above reproach, the husband of one wife, temperate, prudent, respectable, hospitable, able to teach, not addicted to wine or pugnacious, but gentle, peaceable, free from the love of money. He must be one who manages his own household well, keeping his children under control with all dignity (but if a man does not know how to manage his own household, how will he take care of the church of God?), and not a new convert, so that he will not become conceited and fall into the condemnation incurred by the devil. And he must have a good reputation with those outside the church, so that he will not fall into reproach and the snare of the devil. 1 Timothy 3:1-7

7. God Will Judge Us

- For judgment will be merciless to one who has shown no mercy; mercy triumphs over judgment. James 2:13

- Therefore you have no excuse, everyone of you who passes judgment, for in that which you judge another, you condemn yourself; for you who judge practice the same things. Romans 2:1

- Nations will see and be ashamed / Of all their might. / They will put their hand on their mouth, / Their ears will be deaf. / They will lick the dust like a serpent, / Like reptiles of the earth. / They will come trembling out of their fortresses; To the Lord our God they will come in dread / And they will be afraid before You. / Who is a God like You, who pardons iniquity / And passes over the rebellious act of the remnant of His possession? / He does not retain His anger forever, / Because He delights in unchanging love. / He will again have compassion on us; / He will tread our iniquities under foot. / Yes, You will cast all their sins / Into the depths of the sea. / You will give truth to Jacob / And unchanging love to Abraham, / Which You swore to our forefathers / From the days of old. Micah 7:16-20

Summary of What We Are to Know

There is a lot in this last and the next section. It all starts with having respect for God's authority and understanding that respect will be tested at times. We are to learn virtuous models for behavior and then internalize them through effort and practice, eventually becoming good in the process. For in the end, we will each be judged by the same standard we set for others. Therefore, virtues such as mercy, forgiveness, and love will triumph over our judgement of others. Finally, we are to be content with what we produce with our own labor and enjoy its fruits. This is the very opposite of progressive ideas which strive to reach an equality of outcomes as it is a focus on the material over the eternal.

What We Are to Do

1. <u>Be Transformed</u>

    - And do not be conformed to this world, but be transformed by the renewing of your mind, so that you may prove what the will of God is, that which is good and acceptable and perfect. Romans 12:2 (also Hebrews 10:26)

    - But as for you, brethren, do not grow weary of doing good. 2 Thessalonians 3:13 (also James 3:13)

2. <u>Have Faith</u>

    - Behold, as for the proud one, / His soul is not right within him; / But the righteous will live by his faith. Habakkuk 2:4

    - By faith we understand that the worlds were prepared by the word of God, so that what is seen was not made out of things which are visible. Hebrews 11:3

    - And without faith it is impossible to please Him, for he who comes to God must believe that He is and that He is a rewarder of those who seek Him. Hebrews 11:6

3. <u>Use Our Spiritual Gifts</u>

    - For I will pour out water on the thirsty land / And streams on the dry ground; / I will pour out My Spirit on your offspring / And My blessing on your descendants; / And they will spring up among the grass / Like poplars by streams of water. / This one will say, "I am the Lord's"; / And that one will call on the name of Jacob; / And another will write on his hand, "Belonging to the Lord," / And will name Israel's name with honor. Isaiah 44:3-5

    - Now you are Christ's body, and individually members of it. And God has appointed in the church, first apostles, second prophets, third teachers, then miracles, then gifts of healings, helps, administrations, various kinds of tongues. All are not apostles, are they? All are not prophets, are they? All are not teachers, are they? All are not workers of miracles, are they? All do not have gifts of healings, do they? All do not speak with tongues, do they? All do not interpret, do they? But earnestly desire the greater gifts. And I show you a still more excellent way. 1 Corinthians 12:27-31

4. <u>Be Obedient</u>

- Circumcision is nothing, and uncircumcision is nothing, but what matters is the keeping of the commandments of God. 1 Corinthians 7:19 (also Deuteronomy 6:16-8, Ecclesiastes 12:13-4)

- The King will answer and say to them, "Truly I say to you, to the extent that you did it to one of these brothers of Mine, even the least of them, you did it to Me." Matthew 25:40

- But we know that the Law is good, if one uses it lawfully, realizing the fact that law is not made for a righteous person, but for those who are lawless and rebellious, for the ungodly and sinners, for the unholy and profane, for those who kill their fathers or mothers, for murderers and immoral men and homosexuals and kidnappers and liars and perjurers, and whatever else is contrary to sound teaching, according to the glorious gospel of the blessed God, with which I have been entrusted. 1 Timothy 1:8-11

5. <u>Educate Others</u>

- "Hear, O Israel! The Lord is our God, the Lord is one! You shall love the Lord your God with all your heart and with all your soul and with all your might. These words, which I am commanding you today, shall be on your heart. You shall teach them diligently to your sons and shall talk of them when you sit in your house and when you walk by the way and when you lie down and when you rise up. Deuteronomy 6:4-7

- Prescribe and teach these things. Let no one look down on your youthfulness, but rather in speech, conduct, love, faith and purity, show yourself an example of those who believe. 1 Timothy 4:11-2

<u>Summary of What We Are to Do</u>

We are to begin in faith. Faith cannot be proven; it can only be defended. This requires education, and it is the parents' responsibility to educate their children—this responsibility is too important to entrust to government. Publicly funded education of children is a pagan notion coming from Greek philosophy and is intended for a society where people exist to serve their government rather than the other way around as in our society.[2] We are to use our spiritual gifts in our efforts to serve others, whatever those gifts are. By those efforts we will be obedient and also be transformed.

The next chapter examines some rights and responsibilities having their basis in man's actions. At the heart of these rights is man's special nature and the relationship we are each to have with God, as laid out in this chapter.

Chapter 3

Actions

This chapter's focus is the relationship between our actions and purpose, and builds on the previous chapter's contents about man's nature. As part of God's creation, man has many things he shares with it. We are born, die, feed (eat and drink), rest, procreate, experience fear at the unknown, and generally protect our group.

These are things all creation does which together comprise the "laws of nature." But man was also created differently. He was given the ability to reason. This sets man apart from the rest of nature. We're not just called to do these things like the rest of creation does, but to first know and then do in a specific way based upon that underlying knowledge. When we do good, we fulfill our purpose. It's that simple.

However, it is not our works that fulfill our purpose. We do because we know, respect, and observe God's instructions for us. We do not just do by our own will, nor do we just know without doing. We are not saved by our good works, but rather our good works are a reflection of what we believe and follow—an idea. It is that belief, accompanied by actions in serving others out of love, that transforms us into who we are to be and thereby fulfills our purpose.

Acquiring knowledge orienting us toward God depends on understanding our relationship with Him, His requirements for us, developing virtue, and knowing our purpose. We have a duty to fulfill the purpose for which we were created, but we cannot do that without the knowledge that comes from education, the virtues learned and developed through our choices, and the freedom needed for us to make our own choices. Education is required as we are not born with knowledge or virtue, only the freedom to choose. Without a proper education, man turns toward himself and acts to serve himself rather than others, thereby failing to fulfill his purpose.

We therefore have a right to education (to know) and the freedom to choose (to do), and those two rights come with corresponding duties to obey and respect the truth in what we learn and those who have authority over us. Practicing virtuous models of behavior leads to performing acts of charity and fulfilling our purpose. The education being discussed is the very opposite of the secular education provided by our public schools today, an education that is at odds with our serving God by serving others as it has removed anything related to God altogether from its curriculum.

Now to puncture another myth. Fulfilling our purpose requires discerning good from evil: developing and applying the ability to judge. But this judgement is not to be about people, but rather objects such as ideas, decisions, and situations. In short, about the actions we take, the things we do. There is right and wrong, and we all have some basic understanding of that when we are born.

However, our culture today attempts to falsely assert that this knowledge doesn't matter, that these feelings are only sentiments that are not grounded in anything real. This tripe leads to what C.S. Lewis calls "men without chests," a worldview removing man's true nature by separating our reason from our needs. This divides body from soul, making us no more than the rest of creation. It removes our humanity. Both body and soul together are needed to accomplish our purpose.

The relationship between man's nature, knowing, doing, and fulfilling our purpose is diagramed below. We could just as easily call the happiness arising from fulfilling our purpose *joy*. Joy is mentioned over two hundred times in the Bible, and mentioned immediately after love as the good fruit of the spirit.[1]

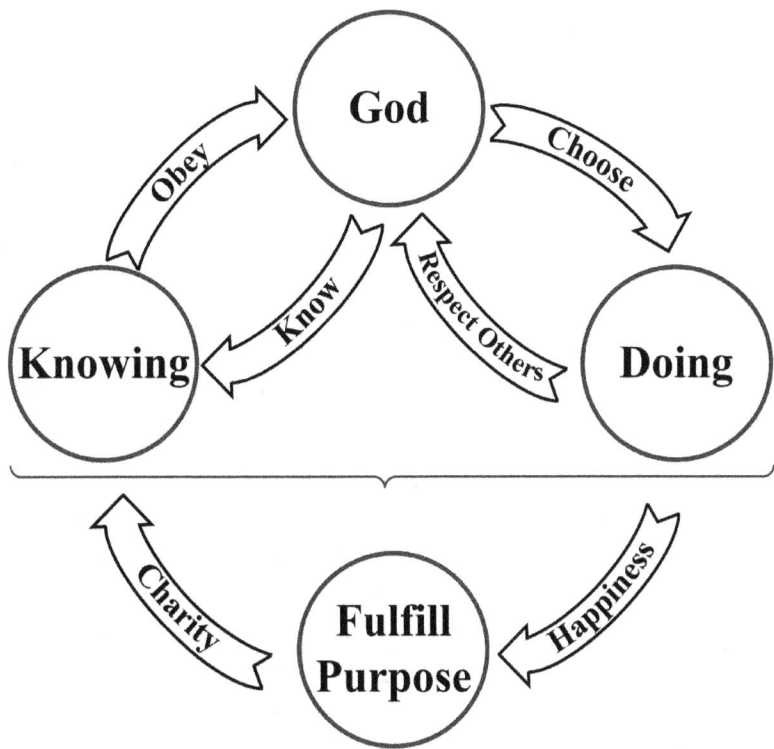

The rights and duties above are laid out in the rest of the chapter.

Knowing

Knowing requires several things: first, understanding knowledge's source; second, accepting what is taught through belief—faith accompanied with respect and obedience to one's teacher; and third, testing what is learned via practice, to discern what is true from what is false. This knowing is to be applied to ourselves, our children, families, and foreigners—in short, to all people. We'll start with several general passages related to the above aspects of knowing before diving deeper into each one.

- Yet we do speak wisdom among those who are mature; a wisdom, however, not of this age nor of the rulers of this age, who are passing away; but we speak God's wisdom in a mystery, the hidden wisdom which God predestined before the ages to our glory; the wisdom which none of the rulers of this age has understood; for if they had understood it they would not have crucified the Lord of glory. 1 Corinthians 2:6-8

- Now this is the commandment, the statutes and the judgments which the Lord your God has commanded me to teach you, that you might do them in the land where you are going over to possess it, so that you and your son and your grandson might fear the Lord your God, to keep all His statutes and His commandments which I command you, all the days of your life, and that your days may be prolonged. Deuteronomy 6:1-2

- By this we know that we have come to know Him, if we keep His commandments. The one who says, "I have come to know Him," and does not keep His commandments, is a liar, and the truth is not in him; but whoever keeps His word, in him the love of God has truly been perfected. By this we know that we are in Him: the one who says he abides in Him ought himself to walk in the same manner as He walked. 1 John 2:3-6

Our Right to Know ...

We are to learn those things necessary to fulfill our purpose. We therefore have a right to be educated in those requirements as we are not born with understanding them. God will assist us in our efforts; we have only to ask. True knowledge comes from God as He is good and truth. His truth does not change nor do the virtues we are to develop, but we do not possess them at birth. Man's knowledge alone is insufficient for achieving our purpose. God's truth provides man with an objective measure, as this comes from outside man. We must both know and do. Our transformation requires us to put others before ourselves, respect them, serve them, and obey them as best we can.

- [Y]ou, therefore, who teach another, do you not teach yourself? You who preach that one shall not steal, do you steal? You who say that one should not commit adultery, do you commit adultery? You who abhor idols, do you rob temples? You who boast in the Law, through your breaking the Law, do you dishonor God? Romans 2:21-3

- For He established a testimony in Jacob / And appointed a law in Israel, / Which He commanded our fathers / That they should teach them to their children, / That the generation to come might know, even the children yet to be born, / That they may arise and tell them to their children, / That they should put their confidence in God / And not forget the works of God, / But keep His commandments. Psalm 78:5-7

- Assemble the people, the men and the women and children and the alien who is in your town, so that they may hear and learn and fear the Lord your God, and be careful to observe all the words of this law. Deuteronomy 31:12-3 (also 2 Chronicles 6:32-4, Ezekiel 44:23-4)

1. <u>God Will Help Us</u>

    - For this commandment which I command you today is not too difficult for you, nor is it out of reach. It is not in heaven, that you should say, "Who will go up to heaven for us to get it for us and make us hear it, that we may observe it?" Nor is it beyond the sea, that you should say, "Who will cross the sea for us to get it for us and make us hear it, that we may observe it?" But the word is very near you, in your mouth and in your heart, that you may observe it. Deuteronomy 30:11-4

    - The spirit of man is the lamp of the Lord, / Searching all the innermost parts of his being. Proverbs 20:27 (also Proverbs 16:9)

    - "For I know the plans that I have for you," declares the Lord, "plans for welfare and not for calamity to give you a future and a hope. Then you will call upon Me and come and pray to Me, and I will listen to you. You will seek Me and find Me when you search for Me with all your heart. I will be found by you," declares the Lord, "and I will restore your fortunes and will gather you from all the nations and from all the places where I have driven you," declares the Lord, "and I will bring you back to the place from where I sent you into exile." Jeremiah 29:11-4

- But if any of you lacks wisdom, let him ask of God, who gives to all generously and without reproach, and it will be given to him. But he must ask in faith without any doubting, for the one who doubts is like the surf of the sea, driven and tossed by the wind. James 1:5-6 (also Matthew 7:7-8 and Luke 11 9-10)

2. True Knowledge Comes from God

- Now we have received, not the spirit of the world, but the Spirit who is from God, so that we may know the things freely given to us by God, which things we also speak, not in words taught by human wisdom, but in those taught by the Spirit, combining spiritual thoughts with spiritual words. 1 Corinthians 2:12-3 (also Malachi 2:5-7)

- By this you know the Spirit of God: every spirit that confesses that Jesus Christ has come in the flesh is from God; and every spirit that does not confess Jesus is not from God; this is the spirit of the antichrist, of which you have heard that it is coming, and now it is already in the world. 1 John 4:2-3 (also 1 John 2:18-23 and 2 John 1:7)

- What was from the beginning, what we have heard, what we have seen with our eyes, what we have looked at and touched with our hands, concerning the Word of Life—and the life was manifested, and we have seen and testify and proclaim to you the eternal life, which was with the Father and was manifested to us—what we have seen and heard we proclaim to you also, so that you too may have fellowship with us; and indeed our fellowship is with the Father, and with His Son Jesus Christ. These things we write, so that our joy may be made complete. 1 John 1:1-4

3. <u>True Knowledge Focuses on the Eternal</u>

- All Scripture is inspired by God and profitable for teaching, for reproof, for correction, for training in righteousness; so that the man of God may be adequate, equipped for every good work. 2 Timothy 3:16-7

- For since the creation of the world His invisible attributes, His eternal power and divine nature, have been clearly seen, being understood through what has been made, so that they are without excuse. Romans 1:20

- And to man He said, "Behold, the fear of the Lord, that is wisdom; / And to depart from evil is understanding." Job 28:28

- Then he said to them, "Watch out! Be on your guard against all kinds of greed; life does not consist in an abundance of possessions." Luke 12:15

4. <u>True Knowledge Focuses on Righteousness</u>

- Finally, brethren, whatever is true, whatever is honorable, whatever is right, whatever is pure, whatever is lovely, whatever is of good repute, if there is any excellence and if anything worthy of praise, dwell on these things. Philippians 4:8

- The beginning of wisdom is: Acquire wisdom; / And with all your acquiring, get understanding. / Prize her, and she will exalt you; / She will honor you if you embrace her. / She will place on your head a garland of grace; / She will present you with a crown of beauty. Proverbs 4:7-9

5. <u>Knowledge Requires Discernment</u>

- So give Your servant an understanding heart to judge Your people to discern between good and evil. For who is able to judge this great people of Yours?" 1 Kings 3:9 (also 1 Kings 3:11-2)

- Teach me good discernment and knowledge, / For I believe in Your commandments. Psalm 119:66

- And this I pray, that your love may abound still more and more in real knowledge and all discernment, so that you may approve the things that are excellent, in order to be sincere and blameless until the day of Christ. Philippians 1:9-10

6. <u>Man's Knowledge is Insufficient</u>

- See to it that no one takes you captive through philosophy and empty deception, according to the tradition of men, according to the elementary principles of the world, rather than according to Christ. Colossians 2:8 (also Romans 8:5)

- For what I am doing, I do not understand; for I am not practicing what I would like to do, but I am doing the very thing I hate. But if I do the very thing I do not want to do, I agree with the Law, confessing that the Law is good. So now, no longer am I the one doing it, but sin which dwells in me. Romans 7:15-7

- For through your knowledge he who is weak is ruined, the brother for whose sake Christ died. And so, by sinning against the brethren and wounding their conscience when it is weak, you sin against Christ. 1 Corinthians 8:11-2

7. <u>Do Not Submit to Man's Teachings</u>

- If you have died with Christ to the elementary principles of the world, why, as if you were living in the world, do you submit yourself to decrees, such as, "Do not handle, do not taste, do not touch!" (which all refer to things destined to perish with use)—in accordance with the commandments and teachings of men? These are matters which have, to be sure, the appearance of wisdom in self-made religion and self-abasement and severe treatment of the body, but are of no value against fleshly indulgence. Colossians 2:20-3 (also Deuteronomy 4:8-9)

- Concerning evil, both hands do it well. / The prince asks, also the judge, for a bribe, / And a great man speaks the desire of his soul; / So they weave it together. / The best of them is like a briar, / The most upright like a thorn hedge. / The day when you post your watchmen, / Your punishment will come. / Then their confusion will occur. Micah 7:3-4

- For the wrath of God is revealed from heaven against all ungodliness and unrighteousness of men who suppress the truth in unrighteousness, because that which is known about God is evident within them; for God made it evident to them. Romans 1:18-9

- For they exchanged the truth of God for a lie, and worshiped and served the creature rather than the Creator, who is blessed forever. Amen. Romans 1:25 (also Romans 1:32)

8. Rejecting God's Knowledge Leads to Man's Destruction

- My people are destroyed for lack of knowledge. / Because you have rejected knowledge, / I also will reject you from being My priest. / Since you have forgotten the law of your God, / I also will forget your children. Hosea 4:6 (also Jeremiah 32:33)

- There is a way which seems right to a man, / But its end is the way of death. Proverbs 16:25

9. Knowledge Must be Combined with Love

- Now concerning things sacrificed to idols, we know that we all have knowledge. Knowledge makes arrogant, but love edifies. If anyone supposes that he knows anything, he has not yet known as he ought to know; but if anyone loves God, he is known by Him. 1 Corinthians 8:1-3 (also Proverbs 10:12)

- On the other hand, I am writing a new commandment to you, which is true in Him and in you, because the darkness is passing away and the true Light is already shining. The one who says he is in the Light and yet hates his brother is in the darkness until now. The one who loves his brother abides in the Light and there is no cause for stumbling in him. But the one who hates his brother is in the darkness and walks in the darkness, and does not know where he is going because the darkness has blinded his eyes. 1 John 2:8-11 (also 1 Thessalonians 4:9)

- By this we know that we love the children of God, when we love God and observe His commandments. For this is the love of God, that we keep His commandments; and His commandments are not burdensome. 1 John 5:2-3

10. Knowledge Must be Combined with Acts

- For if anyone is a hearer of the word and not a doer, he is like a man who looks at his natural face in a mirror; for once he has looked at himself and gone away, he has immediately forgotten what kind of person he was. But one who looks intently at the perfect law, the law of liberty, and abides by it, not having become a forgetful hearer but an effectual doer, this man will be blessed in what he does. James 1:23-5

- If we say that we have fellowship with Him and yet walk in the darkness, we lie and do not practice the truth; but if we walk in the Light as He Himself is in the Light, we have fellowship with one another, and the blood of Jesus His Son cleanses us from all sin. 1 John 1:6-7

11. God's Knowledge Leads to Our Transformation

- A disciple is not above his teacher, nor a slave above his master. It is enough for the disciple that he become like his teacher, and the slave like his master. If they have called the head of the house Beelzebub, how much more will they malign the members of his household! Matthew 10:24-5

- Therefore the Law has become our tutor to lead us to Christ, so that we may be justified by faith. Galatians 3:24

- As a result, we are no longer to be children, tossed here and there by waves and carried about by every wind of doctrine, by the trickery of men, by craftiness in deceitful scheming; but speaking the truth in love, we are to grow up in all aspects into Him who is the head, even Christ. Ephesians 4:14-5

... And Duty to Obey

1. <u>Obedience Comes from Love</u>

- If you love Me, you will keep My commandments. John 14:15 (also John 15:10)

2. <u>Man Must Die to Himself</u>

- Truly, truly, I say to you, unless a grain of wheat falls into the earth and dies, it remains alone; but if it dies, it bears much fruit. He who loves his life loses it, and he who hates his life in this world will keep it to life eternal. If anyone serves Me, he must follow Me; and where I am, there My servant will be also; if anyone serves Me, the Father will honor him. John 12:24-6 (also Mark 8:34-7 and Matthew 16:24-7)

3. <u>We Are Forgiven Through Repentance</u>

- And rend your heart and not your garments. / Now return to the Lord your God, / For He is gracious and compassionate, / Slow to anger, abounding in lovingkindness / And relenting of evil. / Who knows whether He will not turn and relent / And leave a blessing behind Him, / Even a grain offering and a drink offering / For the Lord your God? Joel 2:13-4

- For if you truly amend your ways and your deeds, if you truly practice justice between a man and his neighbor, if you do not oppress the alien, the orphan, or the widow, and do not shed innocent blood in this place, nor walk after other gods to your own ruin, then I will let you dwell in this place, in the land that I gave to your fathers forever and ever. Jeremiah 7:5-7

- And Jesus answered and said to them, "It is not those who are well who need a physician, but those who are sick. I have not come to call the righteous but sinners to repentance." Luke 5:31-2 (also Matthew 9:13)

4. To Obey As Individuals

- He has told you, O man, what is good; / And what does the Lord require of you / But to do justice, to love kindness, / And to walk humbly with your God? Micah 6:8

- But Peter and the apostles answered, "We must obey God rather than men." Acts 5:29

- Thus says the Lord, / "Cursed is the man who trusts in mankind / And makes flesh his strength, / And whose heart turns away from the Lord. / For he will be like a bush in the desert / And will not see when prosperity comes, / But will live in stony wastes in the wilderness, / A land of salt without inhabitant." Jeremiah 17:5-6

5. And Obey As a People

- But He knew their thoughts and said to them, "Any kingdom divided against itself is laid waste; and a house divided against itself falls. If Satan also is divided against himself, how will his kingdom stand? For you say that I cast out demons by Beelzebub. And if I by Beelzebub cast out demons, by whom do your sons cast them out? So they will be your judges. But if I cast out demons by the finger of God, then the kingdom of God has come upon you. Luke 11:17-20 (also Mark 3:24 and Matthew 12:22-7)

- But this is what I commanded them, saying, "Obey My voice, and I will be your God, and you will be My people; and you will walk in all the way which I command you, that it may be well with you." Jeremiah 7:23 (also James 4:7-8; Jeremiah 17:7-8, 32:39-41; and Leviticus 18:2-4)

Summary

Once we learn about our Creator, whose governance we are under, we have a duty to comply with His commands. We have the free will to choose otherwise, but disobedience is not right—it is not virtuous—and therefore is contrary to man's purpose. True knowledge comes from God; man's knowledge is insufficient as man can only know about God what He has chosen to reveal to us through His revelations, His creation, and His image within every one of us.

Knowledge alone is insufficient; it must be accompanied by actions: service performed out of love. These actions do several things. First, they develop our ability to discern between good and evil, and that discernment to instilling virtues. Second, all virtues end in actions that are charity and therefore fulfill our purpose. Third, these actions transform us; we become better than who we were before.

This duty to obey is at two levels: first, as individuals for the decisions we each make every day; and second, as a people who recognize a common set of requirements (commands, rules, rights, etc.) and share a commitment to support the common good through individual actions whose goal is to better society.

Doing

We have the right to make our own choices, a gift from God, but that right must be tempered by knowledge. Our ability to act is not unlimited. We are to act out of love, serving others because it is right. To do this we must receive and accept the knowledge just outlined, thereby acting in a way that does not harm another or infringe upon their rights. Some general passages regarding our actions follow.

- Let all that you do be done in love. 1 Corinthians 16:14

- Let no one seek his own good, but that of his neighbor. 1 Corinthians 10:24

- Little children, make sure no one deceives you; the one who practices righteousness is righteous, just as He is righteous; the one who practices sin is of the devil; for the devil has sinned from the beginning. The Son of God appeared for this purpose, to destroy the works of the devil. 1 John 3:7-8

- Now this I say, he who sows sparingly will also reap sparingly, and he who sows bountifully will also reap bountifully. Each one must do just as he has purposed in his heart, not grudgingly or under compulsion, for God loves a cheerful giver. 2 Corinthians 9:6-7

Our Right to Choose ...

We are to learn and seek good. Our choices transform us, for the better or worse, depending on what we choose. The company we keep also influences our choices. These choices are ours to make, and we are accountable for them. Choosing good leads to our benefit, while choosing what is not good harms us. We can only choose to do either good or evil. There are no other choices, despite what we may tell ourselves. What we learn creates understanding, and that understanding leads us to a duty to serve and obey.

- Seek good and not evil, that you may live; / And thus may the Lord God of hosts be with you, / Just as you have said! / Hate evil, love good, / And establish justice in the gate! / Perhaps the Lord God of hosts / May be gracious to the remnant of Joseph. / Therefore thus says the Lord God of hosts, the Lord, / "There is wailing in all the plazas, / And in all the streets they say, 'Alas! Alas!' / They also call the farmer to mourning / And professional mourners to lamentation." Amos 5:14-6

- So speak and so act as those who are to be judged by the law of liberty. James 2:12

- "These are the things you are to do: Speak the truth to each other, and render true and sound judgment in your courts; do not plot evil against each other, and do not love to swear falsely. I hate all this," declares the Lord. Zechariah 8:16-7

1. Freedom Comes from God

   - Jesus answered them, "Truly, truly, I say to you, everyone who commits sin is the slave of sin. The slave does not remain in the house forever; the son does remain forever. So if the Son makes you free, you will be free indeed. John 8:34-6 (also Romans 8:2)

   - So also we, while we were children, were held in bondage under the elemental things of the world. But when the fullness of the time came, God sent forth His Son, born of a woman, born under the Law, so that He might redeem those who were under the Law, that we might receive the adoption as sons. Because you are sons, God has sent forth the Spirit of His Son into our hearts, crying, "Abba! Father!" Therefore you are no longer a slave, but a son; and if a son, then an heir through God. Galatians 4:3-7

   - For he who was called in the Lord while a slave, is the Lord's freedman; likewise he who was called while free, is Christ's slave. You were bought with a price; do not become slaves of men. 1 Corinthians 7:22-3

2. We Are Transformed by Our Choices

   - Now the Lord is the Spirit, and where the Spirit of the Lord is, there is liberty. But we all, with unveiled face, beholding as in a mirror the glory of the Lord, are being transformed into the same image from glory to glory, just as from the Lord, the Spirit. 2 Corinthians 3:17-8

   - And just as they did not see fit to acknowledge God any longer, God gave them over to a depraved mind, to do those things which are not proper, being filled with all unrighteousness, wickedness, greed, evil; full of envy, murder, strife, deceit, malice; they are gossips, slanderers, haters of God, insolent, arrogant, boastful, inventors of evil, disobedient to parents, without understanding, untrustworthy, unloving, unmerciful. Romans 1:28-32

3. And So Should Keep Good Company

- Do not be deceived: "Bad company corrupts good morals." 1 Corinthians 15:31

- Do not be bound together with unbelievers; for what partnership have righteousness and lawlessness, or what fellowship has light with darkness? Or what harmony has Christ with Belial, or what has a believer in common with an unbeliever? 2 Corinthians 6:14-5

- Do not be envious of evil men, / Nor desire to be with them. Proverbs 24:1

4. And Choose To Do Good

- Therefore be imitators of God, as beloved children; and walk in love, just as Christ also loved you and gave Himself up for us, an offering and a sacrifice to God as a fragrant aroma. Ephesians 5:1-2

- Let love be without hypocrisy. Abhor what is evil; cling to what is good. Romans 12:9

- So when you spread out your hands in prayer, / I will hide My eyes from you. / Yes, even though you multiply prayers, / I will not listen. / Your hands are covered with blood. / Wash yourselves, make yourselves clean. / Remove the evil of your deeds from My sight. / Cease to do evil, / Learn to do good. / Seek justice, / Reprove the ruthless, / Defend the orphan, / Plead for the widow. / "Come now, and let us reason together," / Says the Lord, / "Though your sins are as scarlet, / They will be as white as snow; / Though they are red like crimson, / They will be like wool. / If you consent and obey, / You will eat the best of the land. / But if you refuse and rebel, You will be devoured by the sword." / Truly, the mouth of the Lord has spoken." Isaiah 1:15-20

5. <u>We Should Choose to Serve</u>

- Sitting down, He called the twelve and said to them, "If anyone wants to be first, he shall be last of all and servant of all." Taking a child, He set him before them, and taking him in His arms, He said to them, "Whoever receives one child like this in My name receives Me; and whoever receives Me does not receive Me, but Him who sent Me." Mark 9:35-7 (also Mark 10:31, Mark 10:42-5, Matthew 20:25-8, John 13:12-7)

- In everything, therefore, treat people the same way you want them to treat you, for this is the Law and the Prophets. Matthew 7:12

- For if you forgive others for their transgressions, your heavenly Father will also forgive you. But if you do not forgive others, then your Father will not forgive your transgressions. Matthew 6:14-5

6. <u>Our Faith Leads to Doing Good</u>

- What use is it, my brethren, if someone says he has faith but he has no works? Can that faith save him? If a brother or sister is without clothing and in need of daily food, and one of you says to them, "Go in peace, be warmed and be filled," and yet you do not give them what is necessary for their body, what use is that? Even so faith, if it has no works, is dead, being by itself. But someone may well say, "You have faith and I have works; show me your faith without the works, and I will show you my faith by my works." James 2:14-8

- Let your light shine before men in such a way that they may see your good works, and glorify your Father who is in heaven. Matthew 5:16

7. <u>We Are To Do No Injustice</u>

- You shall do no injustice in judgment; you shall not be partial to the poor nor defer to the great, but you are to judge your neighbor fairly. You shall not go about as a slanderer among your people, and you are not to act against the life of your neighbor; I am the Lord. Leviticus 19:15-6 (also Deuteronomy 32:3-5)

- What shall we say then? There is no injustice with God, is there? May it never be! For He says to Moses, "I will have mercy on whom I have mercy, and I will have compassion on whom I have compassion." Romans 9:14-5

8. <u>Man Is Responsible for his Choices</u>

- Let no one say when he is tempted, "I am being tempted by God"; for God cannot be tempted by evil, and He Himself does not tempt anyone. But each one is tempted when he is carried away and enticed by his own lust. Then when lust has conceived, it gives birth to sin; and when sin is accomplished, it brings forth death. Do not be deceived, my beloved brethren. James 1:13-6

- What is the source of quarrels and conflicts among you? Is not the source your pleasures that wage war in your members? You lust and do not have; so you commit murder. You are envious and cannot obtain; so you fight and quarrel. You do not have because you do not ask. You ask and do not receive, because you ask with wrong motives, so that you may spend it on your pleasures. You adulteresses, do you not know that friendship with the world is hostility toward God? Therefore whoever wishes to be a friend of the world makes himself an enemy of God. James 4:1-4

9. <u>Our Bad Choices Harm Us</u>

- There is nothing outside the man which can defile him if it goes into him; but the things which proceed out of the man are what defile the man. Mark 7:15 (also Mark 7:18-23 and Matthew 15:17-20)

- Now the deeds of the flesh are evident, which are: immorality, impurity, sensuality, idolatry, sorcery, enmities, strife, jealousy, outbursts of anger, disputes, dissensions, factions, envying, drunkenness, carousing, and things like these, of which I forewarn you, just as I have forewarned you, that those who practice such things will not inherit the kingdom of God. But the fruit of the Spirit is love, joy, peace, patience, kindness, goodness, faithfulness, gentleness, self-control; against such things there is no law. Galatians 5:19-23 (also Colossians 3:5-9)

- Jesus said to his disciples: "Things that cause people to stumble are bound to come, but woe to anyone through whom they come. It would be better for them to be thrown into the sea with a millstone tied around their neck than to cause one of these little ones to stumble. So watch yourselves. If your brother or sister sins against you, rebuke them; and if they repent, forgive them. Even if they sin against you seven times in a day and seven times come back to you saying 'I repent,' you must forgive them." Luke 17:1-4

10. Our Bad Choices Are Contrary to God's Will for Us

- He who is not with Me is against Me; and he who does not gather with Me scatters. Matthew 12:30 (also Luke 11:23)

- See, I am setting before you today a blessing and a curse: the blessing, if you listen to the commandments of the Lord your God, which I am commanding you today; and the curse, if you do not listen to the commandments of the Lord your God, but turn aside from the way which I am commanding you today, by following other gods which you have not known. Deuteronomy 11:26-8

- But to the wicked God says, / "What right have you to tell of My statutes / And to take My covenant in your mouth? / For you hate discipline, / And you cast My words behind you. / When you see a thief, you are pleased with him, / And you associate with adulterers. / You let your mouth loose in evil / And your tongue frames deceit. / You sit and speak against your brother; / You slander your own mother's son. / These things you have done and I kept silence; / You thought that I was just like you; / I will reprove you and state the case in order before your eyes. / Now consider this, you who forget God, / Or I will tear you in pieces, and there will be none to deliver." Psalm 50:16-22

11. We Can Only Choose Good or Evil

- No one can serve two masters; for either he will hate the one and love the other, or he will be devoted to one and despise the other. You cannot serve God and wealth. Matthew 6:24

- Whoever can be trusted with very little can also be trusted with much, and whoever is dishonest with very little will also be dishonest with much. So if you have not been trustworthy in handling worldly wealth, who will trust you with true riches? And if you have not been trustworthy with someone else's property, who will give you property of your own? No one can serve two masters. Either you will hate the one and love the other, or you will be devoted to the one and despise the other. You cannot serve both God and money. Luke 16:10-3

... And Responsibility to Respect Others

1. God

- The fear of the Lord is the beginning of wisdom; / A good understanding have all those who do His commandments; / His praise endures forever. Psalm 111:10 (also Proverbs 1:7, 9:10)

- For in Him [Christ] all the fullness of Deity dwells in bodily form, and in Him you have been made complete, and He is the head over all rule and authority. Colossians 2:9-10

- Therefore if God gave to them [the Gentiles] the same gift as He gave to us also after believing in the Lord Jesus Christ, who was I that I could stand in God's way?" When they heard this, they quieted down and glorified God, saying, "Well then, God has granted to the Gentiles also the repentance that leads to life." Acts 11:17-8

2. <u>Ourselves</u>

- For you yourselves know how you ought to follow our example, because we did not act in an undisciplined manner among you, nor did we eat anyone's bread without paying for it, but with labor and hardship we kept working night and day so that we would not be a burden to any of you; not because we do not have the right to this, but in order to offer ourselves as a model for you, so that you would follow our example. For even when we were with you, we used to give you this order: if anyone is not willing to work, then he is not to eat, either. For we hear that some among you are leading an undisciplined life, doing no work at all, but acting like busybodies. 2 Thessalonians 3:7-11

- Make sure that your character is free from the love of money, being content with what you have; for He Himself has said, "I will never desert you, nor will I ever forsake you," so that we confidently say, "The Lord is my helper, I will not be afraid. What will man do to me?" Hebrews 13:5-6

- But each one must examine his own work, and then he will have reason for boasting in regard to himself alone, and not in regard to another. For each one will bear his own load. Galatians 6:4-5

- For the Lord God helps Me, / Therefore, I am not disgraced; / Therefore, I have set My face like flint, / And I know that I will not be ashamed. Isaiah 50:7

3. Children

- Children, obey your parents in the Lord, for this is right. Honor your father and mother (which is the first commandment with a promise), so that it may be well with you, and that you may live long on the earth. Ephesians 6:1-3

- The rod and reproof give wisdom, / But a child who gets his own way brings shame to his mother. / When the wicked increase, transgression increases; / But the righteous will see their fall. / Correct your son, and he will give you comfort; / He will also delight your soul. / Where there is no vision, the people are unrestrained, / But happy is he who keeps the law. Proverbs 29:15-8

4. Wives

- In the same way, you wives, be submissive to your own husbands so that even if any of them are disobedient to the word, they may be won without a word by the behavior of their wives, as they observe your chaste and respectful behavior. Your adornment must not be merely external—braiding the hair, and wearing gold jewelry, or putting on dresses; but let it be the hidden person of the heart, with the imperishable quality of a gentle and quiet spirit, which is precious in the sight of God. 1 Peter 3:1-4

- Wives, be subject to your own husbands, as to the Lord. For the husband is the head of the wife, as Christ also is the head of the church, He Himself being the Savior of the body. But as the church is subject to Christ, so also the wives ought to be to their husbands in everything. Ephesians 5:22-3

5. Husbands

- Fathers, do not provoke your children to anger, but bring them up in the discipline and instruction of the Lord. Ephesians 6:4

- Husbands, love your wives, just as Christ also loved the church and gave Himself up for her, so that He might sanctify her, having cleansed her by the washing of water with the word, that He might present to Himself the church in all her glory, having no spot or wrinkle or any such thing; but that she would be holy and blameless. So husbands ought also to love their own wives as their own bodies. He who loves his own wife loves himself; for no one ever hated his own flesh, but nourishes and cherishes it, just as Christ also does the church, because we are members of His body. For this reason a man shall leave his father and mother and shall be joined to his wife, and the two shall become one flesh. Ephesians 5:24-31

- You husbands in the same way, live with your wives in an understanding way, as with someone weaker, since she is a woman; and show her honor as a fellow heir of the grace of life, so that your prayers will not be hindered. To sum up, all of you be harmonious, sympathetic, brotherly, kindhearted, and humble in spirit; not returning evil for evil or insult for insult, but giving a blessing instead; for you were called for the very purpose that you might inherit a blessing. For, "The one who desires life, to love and see good days, must keep his tongue from evil and his lips from speaking deceit. He must turn away from evil and do good; he must seek peace and pursue it. For the eyes of the Lord are toward the righteous, and His ears attend to their prayer, but the face of the Lord is against those who do evil." 1 Peter 3:7-12

6. Those in Authority

- Submit yourselves for the Lord's sake to every human institution, whether to a king as the one in authority, or to governors as sent by him for the punishment of evildoers and the praise of those who do right. For such is the will of God that by doing right you may silence the ignorance of foolish men. Act as free men, and do not use your freedom as a covering for evil, but use it as bondslaves of God. Honor all people, love the brotherhood, fear God, honor the king. 1 Peter 2:13-7

- First of all, then, I urge that entreaties and prayers, petitions and thanksgivings, be made on behalf of all men, for kings and all who are in authority, so that we may lead a tranquil and quiet life in all godliness and dignity. This is good and acceptable in the sight of God our Savior, who desires all men to be saved and to come to the knowledge of the truth. 1 Timothy 2:1-4

- Servants, be submissive to your masters with all respect, not only to those who are good and gentle, but also to those who are unreasonable. For this finds favor, if for the sake of conscience toward God a person bears up under sorrows when suffering unjustly. For what credit is there if, when you sin and are harshly treated, you endure it with patience? But if when you do what is right and suffer for it you patiently endure it, this finds favor with God. 1 Peter 2:18-20

Summary

Actions encompass many daily decisions about what we do, including the company we keep. Good company reinforces virtuous knowledge and behavior. Choosing what is not good is not only contrary to God's will for us, but leads to our destruction. We can only choose to do good or evil, and we alone are each responsible for our choices.

In making our choices, we owe a duty to others as outlined in the last section. As God is creation's governor, we owe a duty to obey His will. We further owe a duty to other people not to make choices that please only us and deprives them of some portion of their rights. Finally, there are relationships within society where one person has a special role that we have a duty to respect and acknowledge in our actions. Examples of these types of relationships include children and parents, spouses in a marriage, and government and its citizens.

Both knowing and doing have a common theme, whether man fulfills his purpose or not. Man's purpose is fulfilled through the transformation occurring by doing good. It is to our purpose that we now turn.

Fulfilling Our Purpose

We were specially made to fulfill a specific purpose: to become good. A number of things we've already discussed contribute to our effort: applying ourselves to the education opportunities we receive; internalizing the models of virtuous behavior we learn; and applying effort to practice what we've learned through the choices we make.

We sometimes stumble and fall, but that's okay. What matters is our reaction to failing. Do we learn and try again, or just give up? Do we surround ourselves with good people who help us, or with those who tell us not to bother because it doesn't matter?

In the end it is God's love for us—His grace—that makes it possible not to be held accountable for those times when we stumble. It was paid for by someone else on our behalf. If we accept that, then our heart, choices, and actions show others what path we've placed ourselves upon. We'll open this last section with a few verses related to the ideas just presented.

- For He Himself [Christ] is our peace, who made both groups into one and broke down the barrier of the dividing wall, by abolishing in His flesh the enmity, which is the Law of commandments contained in ordinances, so that in Himself He might make the two into one new man, thus establishing peace, and might reconcile them both in one body to God through the cross, by it having put to death the enmity. And He came and preached peace to you who were far away, and peace to those who were near; for through Him we both have our access in one Spirit to the Father. Ephesians 2:14-8

- And the testimony is this, that God has given us eternal life, and this life is in His Son. He who has the Son has the life; he who does not have the Son of God does not have the life. 1 John 5:11-2

- The true light that gives light to everyone was coming into the world. He was in the world, and though the world was made through him, the world did not recognize him. He came to that which was his own, but his own did not receive him. Yet to all who did receive him, to those who believed in his name, he gave the right to become children of God—children born not of natural descent, nor of human decision or a husband's will, but born of God. John 1:9-12

Our Right to Happiness ...

Our right to happiness comes from God's love for us, a love that is open to each and every one of us to accept and receive. Following are passages about the love and contentment we are to have, how we are to serve, and whom we are to serve.

1. <u>We Are Loved By God</u>

- But now, thus says the Lord, your Creator, O Jacob, / And He who formed you, O Israel, / "Do not fear, for I have redeemed you; / I have called you by name; you are Mine! / When you pass through the waters, I will be with you; / And through the rivers, they will not overflow you. / When you walk through the fire, you will not be scorched, / Nor will the flame burn you. / For I am the Lord your God, / The Holy One of Israel, your Savior; / I have given Egypt as your ransom, / Cush and Seba in your place. / Since you are precious in My sight, / Since you are honored and I love you, / I will give other men in your place and other peoples in exchange for your life. / Do not fear, for I am with you; / I will bring your offspring from the east, / And gather you from the west. / I will say to the north, 'Give them up!' / And to the south, 'Do not hold them back.' / Bring My sons from afar / And my daughters from the ends of the earth, / Everyone who is called by My name, / And whom I have created for My glory, / Whom I have formed, even whom I have made." Isaiah 43:1-7

- Beloved, let us love one another, for love is from God; and everyone who loves is born of God and knows God. The one who does not love does not know God, for God is love. By this the love of God was manifested in us, that God has sent His only begotten Son into the world so that we might live through Him. In this is love, not that we loved God, but that He loved us and sent His Son to be the propitiation for our sins. 1 John 4:7-10 (also Romans 5:8)

- For you know the grace of our Lord Jesus Christ, that though He was rich, yet for your sake He became poor, so that you through His poverty might become rich. 2 Corinthians 8:9

2. And Redeemed by Grace

- A highway will be there, a roadway, / And it will be called the Highway of Holiness. / The unclean will not travel on it, / But it will be for him who walks that way, / And fools will not wander on it. / No lion will be there, / Nor will any vicious beast go up on it; / These will not be found there. / But the redeemed will walk there, / And the ransomed of the Lord will return / And come with joyful shouting to Zion, / With everlasting joy upon their heads. / They will find gladness and joy, / And sorrow and sighing will flee away. Isaiah 35:8-10

- For I am not ashamed of the gospel, for it is the power of God for salvation to everyone who believes, to the Jew first and also to the Greek. For in it the righteousness of God is revealed from faith to faith; as it is written, "But the righteous man shall live by faith." Romans 1:16-7

3. The Love Man is to Have

- Love never fails; but if there are gifts of prophecy, they will be done away; if there are tongues, they will cease; if there is knowledge, it will be done away. For we know in part and we prophesy in part; but when the perfect comes, the partial will be done away. When I was a child, I used to speak like a child, think like a child, reason like a child; when I became a man, I did away with childish things. For now we see in a mirror dimly, but then face to face; now I know in part, but then I will know fully just as I also have been fully known. But now faith, hope, love, abide these three; but the greatest of these is love. 1 Corinthians 13:8-13 (also 2 Peter 4:8-10)

- This is His commandment, that we believe in the name of His Son Jesus Christ, and love one another, just as He commanded us. The one who keeps His commandments abides in Him, and He in him. We know by this that He abides in us, by the Spirit whom He has given us. 1 John 3:23-4 (also 1 John 4:20-1)

- Do not love the world nor the things in the world. If anyone loves the world, the love of the Father is not in him. For all that is in the world, the lust of the flesh and the lust of the eyes and the boastful pride of life, is not from the Father, but is from the world. 1 John 2:15-6

4. The Character Man is to Have

- For by these He has granted to us His precious and magnificent promises, so that by them you may become partakers of the divine nature, having escaped the corruption that is in the world by lust. Now for this very reason also, applying all diligence, in your faith supply moral excellence, and in your moral excellence, knowledge, and in your knowledge, self-control, and in your self-control, perseverance, and in your perseverance, godliness, and in your godliness, brotherly kindness, and in your brotherly kindness, love. For if these qualities are yours and are increasing, they render you neither useless nor unfruitful in the true knowledge of our Lord Jesus Christ. For he who lacks these qualities is blind or short-sighted, having forgotten his purification from his former sins. 2 Peter 1:4-9

- [Y]ou will be enriched in everything for all liberality, which through us is producing thanksgiving to God. 2 Corinthians 9:11

5. The Contentment Man is to Have

- Go then, eat your bread in happiness and drink your wine with a cheerful heart; for God has already approved your works. Let your clothes be white all the time, and let not oil be lacking on your head. Enjoy life with the woman whom you love all the days of your fleeting life which He has given to you under the sun; for this is your reward in life and in your toil in which you have labored under the sun. Ecclesiastes 9:7-9

- [A]nd constant friction between men of depraved mind and deprived of the truth, who suppose that godliness is a means of gain. But godliness actually is a means of great gain when accompanied by contentment. For we have brought nothing into the world, so we cannot take anything out of it either. 1 Timothy 6:5-7

... And Responsibility to Perform Charitable Acts

If we have voluntarily chosen to serve God, then we have placed ourselves on a path to be obedient to Him, first and foremost. What He asks is simple, but not always easy to do. We are to fulfill our purpose by becoming good. This does require some taking care of ourselves, but its primary focus should be serving others. But we can only do after we truly know. In order to know, we must be able to discern good from evil, or else we will not know how to serve in a way that actually can help another person.

This is what God calls us to do. Not to judge people, but between good and evil instead. Charity is not about the stuff, the material things—that is the way of the world and not God. It comes down to understanding what charity really is, voluntarily serving others by sharing their burden. When we do this, we help someone else become better able to fulfill their purpose, and we grow in virtue and become more capable of fulfilling our purpose as well. Both people grow and become more independent. This is the opposite of what the world professes. Instead, it calls for the redistribution of material things in order to make things 'fair.'

This worldly fairness is the very opposite of what we are called to know and do. It is based not on service, but instead on judging others, theft, and lording power over others. This is vice parading itself as virtue—a caricature of who we are to be. A human attempt to short-cut the process, which always fails. We'll close this chapter with a few passages related to these ideas.

1. <u>God's Judgement</u>

- The law of the Lord is perfect, restoring the soul; / The testimony of the Lord is sure, making wise the simple. / The precepts of the Lord are right, rejoicing the heart; / The commandment of the Lord is pure, enlightening the eyes. / The fear of the Lord is clean, enduring forever; / The judgments of the Lord are true; they are righteous altogether. Psalm 19:7-9

- He who rejects Me and does not receive My sayings, has one who judges him; the word I spoke is what will judge him at the last day. John 12:48 (also John 16:7-11)

- But when the Son of Man comes in His glory, and all the angels with Him, then He will sit on His glorious throne. All the nations will be gathered before Him; and He will separate them from one another, as the shepherd separates the sheep from the goats; and He will put the sheep on His right, and the goats on the left. Matthew 25:31-3 (also Revelations 20:12-5)

2. <u>Do Not Judge Others</u>

- Do not judge according to appearance, but judge with righteous judgment." John 7:24

- Do not speak against one another, brethren. He who speaks against a brother or judges his brother, speaks against the law

- and judges the law; but if you judge the law, you are not a doer of the law but a judge of it. There is only one Lawgiver and Judge, the One who is able to save and to destroy; but who are you who judge your neighbor? James 4:11-2

- To know wisdom and instruction, / To discern the sayings of understanding, / To receive instruction in wise behavior, / Righteousness, justice and equity; / To give prudence to the naive, / To the youth knowledge and discretion, / A wise man will hear and increase in learning, / And a man of understanding will acquire wise counsel, / To understand a proverb and a figure, / The words of the wise and their riddles. Proverbs 1:2-6

- Do not judge so that you will not be judged. For in the way you judge, you will be judged; and by your standard of measure, it will be measured to you. Matthew 7:1-2

3. <u>What is Charity?</u>

- This is My commandment, that you love one another, just as I have loved you. Greater love has no one than this, that one lay down his life for his friends. You are My friends if you do what I command you. John 15:12-4

- [D]o not merely look out for your own personal interests, but also for the interests of others. Philippians 2:4

- Do not withhold good from those to whom it is due, / When it is in your power to do it. / Do not say to your neighbor, "Go, and come back, / And tomorrow I will give it," / When you have it with you. / Do not devise harm against your neighbor, / While he lives securely beside you. / Do not contend with a man without cause, / If he has done you no harm. / Do not envy a man of violence / And do not choose any of his ways. / For the devious are an abomination to the Lord; / But He is intimate with the upright. Proverbs 3:27-32 (also Deuteronomy 15:7-11)

- When you reap your harvest in your field and have forgotten a sheaf in the field, you shall not go back to get it; it shall be for the alien, for the orphan, and for the widow, in order that the Lord your God may bless you in all the work of your hands. When you beat your olive tree, you shall not go over the boughs again; it shall be for the alien, for the orphan, and for the widow. When you gather the grapes of your vineyard, you shall not go over it again; it shall be for the alien, for the orphan, and for the widow. You shall remember that you were a slave in the land of Egypt; therefore I am commanding you to do this thing. Deuteronomy 24:19-22 (also Deuteronomy 23:24-5)

4. <u>Voluntary Service to Others</u>

- Have this attitude in yourselves which was also in Christ Jesus, who, although He existed in the form of God, did not regard equality with God a thing to be grasped, but emptied Himself, taking the form of a bond-servant, and being made in the likeness of men. Being found in appearance as a man, He humbled Himself by becoming obedient to the point of death, even death on a cross. For this reason also, God highly exalted Him, and bestowed on Him the name which is above every name, so that at the name of Jesus every knee will bow, of those who are in heaven and on earth and under the earth, and that every tongue will confess that Jesus Christ is Lord, to the glory of God the Father. Philippians 2:5-11 (also Mark 10:42-5, Matthew 20:25-8, Luke 22:24-7)

- Therefore, I exhort the elders among you, as your fellow elder and witness of the sufferings of Christ, and a partaker also of the glory that is to be revealed, shepherd the flock of God among you, exercising oversight not under compulsion, but voluntarily, according to the will of God; and not for sordid gain, but with eagerness; nor yet as lording it over those allotted to your charge, but proving to be examples to the flock. And when the Chief Shepherd appears, you will receive the unfading crown of glory. You younger men, likewise, be subject to your elders; and all of you, clothe yourselves with humility toward one another, for God is opposed to the proud, but gives grace to the humble. Therefore humble yourselves under the mighty hand of God, that He may exalt you at the proper time, casting all your anxiety on Him, because He cares for you. 1 Peter 5:1-7

- Instruct those who are rich in this present world not to be conceited or to fix their hope on the uncertainty of riches, but on God, who richly supplies us with all things to enjoy. Instruct them to do good, to be rich in good works, to be generous and ready to share, storing up for themselves the treasure of a good foundation for the future, so that they may take hold of that which is life indeed. 1 Timothy 6:17-9

5. To Whom Are We to Show Charity?

- But if anyone does not provide for his own, and especially for those of his household, he has denied the faith and is worse than an unbeliever. 1 Timothy 5:8

- Open your mouth for the mute, / For the rights of all the unfortunate. / Open your mouth, judge righteously, / And defend the rights of the afflicted and needy. Proverbs 31:8-9

- Honor widows who are widows indeed; but if any widow has children or grandchildren, they must first learn to practice piety in regard to their own family and to make some return to their parents; for this is acceptable in the sight of God. Now she who is a widow indeed and who has been left alone, has fixed her hope on God and continues in entreaties and prayers night and day. But she who gives herself to wanton pleasure is dead even while she lives. 1 Timothy 5:3-6

- You shall sow your land for six years and gather in its yield, but on the seventh year you shall let it rest and lie fallow, so that the needy of your people may eat; and whatever they leave

- the beast of the field may eat. You are to do the same with your vineyard and your olive grove. Exodus 23:10-1

- So then, while we have opportunity, let us do good to all people, and especially to those who are of the household of the faith. Galatians 6:10

6. <u>How Are We to Show Charity?</u>

- Bear one another's burdens, and thereby fulfill the law of Christ. Galatians 6:2

- He who steals must steal no longer; but rather he must labor, performing with his own hands what is good, so that he will have something to share with one who has need. Ephesians 4:28

- If any woman who is a believer has dependent widows, she must assist them and the church must not be burdened, so that it may assist those who are widows indeed. 1 Timothy 5:16

- Sell your possessions and give to the poor. Provide purses for yourselves that will not wear out, a treasure in heaven that will never fail, where no thief comes near and no moth destroys. For where your treasure is, there your heart will be also. Luke 12:33-4

- Beware of practicing your righteousness before men to be noticed by them; otherwise you have no reward with your Father who is in heaven. So when you give to the poor, do not sound a trumpet before you, as the hypocrites do in the synagogues and in the streets, so that they may be honored by men. Truly I say to you, they have their reward in full. But when you give to the poor, do not let your left hand know what your right hand is doing, so that your giving will be in secret; and your Father who sees what is done in secret will reward you. When you pray, you are not to be like the hypocrites; for they love to stand and pray in the synagogues and on the street corners so that they may be seen by men. Truly I say to you, they have their reward in full. But you, when you pray, go into your inner room, close your door and pray to your Father who is in secret, and your Father who sees what is done in secret will reward you. Matthew 6:1-6

7. <u>Righteousness Rewarded</u>

- But in all these things we overwhelmingly conquer through Him who loved us. For I am convinced that neither death, nor life, nor angels, nor principalities, nor things present, nor things to come, nor powers, nor height, nor depth, nor any other created thing, will be able to separate us from the love of God, which is in Christ Jesus our Lord. Romans 8:37-9

- Then the King will say to those on His right, "Come, you who are blessed of My Father, inherit the kingdom prepared for you from the foundation of the world. For I was hungry, and you gave Me something to eat; I was thirsty, and you gave Me something to drink; I was a stranger, and you invited Me in; naked, and you clothed Me; I was sick, and you visited Me; I was in prison, and you came to Me." Matthew 25:34-6

Summary

The above passages describe some of the things we are to know and do regarding charity. While charity is the action, love is the affect—the motive. The following characteristics illustrate what this love is to look like.[2]

1. Provide for the poor and those in need (Matthew 6, 19:16-30, Mark 10:17-31, Luke 12:13-34, and 18:18-34)
2. Come from within (Matthew 5, Luke 11)
3. Provide what is needed (Matthew 25:31-46)
4. Give more than what is asked (Matthew 5:38-42 and Luke 6:27-34)
5. Expect nothing in return (Luke 6:35-6)
6. Be revealed by our actions (Matthew 7:24-29 and Luke 6:46-9)

Some virtues associated with charity include the following:

1. Forgiveness (Matthew 18:21-35)
2. Sacrifice (Luke 21:1-9, Romans 5, 2 Corinthians 5, and Ephesians 5)
3. Mercy (Matthew 5:7, 18:21-35, 23:23-4, and Luke 10:30-37)
4. Obedience (John 14, 15, 1 John 2, 5)
5. Concern for others welfare (Romans 13, 15, and Galatians 5 and 6)
6. Love and compassion (1 Corinthians 13)

Finally, charity

1. Is recognized by its fruits (Matthew 7:15-24, 12:33-7, and Luke 6:39-45);
2. Occurs when we are connected to God (John 15 and James 5:7-20).

God loves us so much that while we were yet separated from Him, He sent Christ to die in our place. That is redemption, and it came at the cost of another's life. To ignore that fact is not to be righteous. We are called to show that same kind of love, that agape we discussed back in the first chapter. This kind of love requires virtues, the virtues listed in the passage above from 2 Peter regarding man's character. We are not here to pursue material goods, although that in and of itself is not bad, but are to enjoy whatever we have. We are to enjoy those we love, the things we are able to produce by our labor, and the time we have to share with each other. The end is eternal peace and happiness, and it is freely offered to each of us. All it takes is our acceptance. *Without that acceptance, we avoid the duties we've discussed, and we also lose the benefits from the rights that we each have as we are no longer turned to God.*

We do have a right to true happiness, but that right comes with a duty to do good because we will be judged—a judgement based not only upon our actions, but our hearts. Man is to develop the ability to judge between good and evil, and not our fellow man with whom we share a common nature. Discerning good from evil leads to our transformation, judging others does not. To do that requires using our freedom to serve others in love and not ourselves. It's not about the money or other material things, but instead about providing another what they need as a way of assisting them become independent, capable of fulfilling their purpose. That is why one person's dependence on another creates a type of slavery contrary to our purpose.

There are all kinds of poverty, spiritual as well as material. We are called to help where we can. Sometimes just listening and caring is enough to make a difference for another. In all matters though, we should put on humility (another virtue) as none of us are perfect, and all of us need help at some time or another.

God also gave man dominion over all the plants and animals. This dominion too is derived from man's special nature, and it is to this topic we turn in the next chapter.

Chapter 4

Dominion

We've already touched on dominion several times. Dominion is authority. *Authority rests with the ruler, but can be granted to another to exercise.* When a ruler grants someone dominion, it is accompanied by the duty of stewardship, the responsibility of caring for whatever has been entrusted to them by the ruler. Take the dominion man was given over God's creation. Creation was made for our use, but we do not own it.

Instead, dominion is further evidence of God's goodness. God provides for us; in fact, one of God's names is Jehovah-jireh—*God will provide*. This is also a matter of grace. God loving us, freely giving us not only the gift of existence but providing the means of support for that existence.

Several passages point to God's ownership of all life and the land, His granting dominion over those things to man, and providing for man's continued existence. *Man owns none of these things, but is to use and care for them in meeting his own needs.*

- Every moving thing that is alive shall be food for you; I give all to you, as I gave the green plant. Only you shall not eat flesh with its life, that is, its blood. Surely I will require your lifeblood; from every beast I will require it. And from every man, from every man's brother I will require the life of man. "Whoever sheds man's blood, by man his blood shall be shed, for in the image of God He made man." Genesis 9:3-6

- The land, moreover, shall not be sold permanently, for the land is Mine; for you are but aliens and sojourners with Me. Thus for every piece of your property, you are to provide for the redemption of the land. Leviticus 25:23-4

- "For this reason I say to you, do not be worried about your life, as to what you will eat or what you will drink; nor for your body, as to what you will put on. Is not life more than food, and the body more than clothing? Look at the birds of the air, that they do not sow, nor reap nor gather into barns, and yet your heavenly Father feeds them. Are you not worth much more than they? And who of you by being worried can add a single hour to his life? And why are you worried about clothing? Observe how the lilies of the field grow; they do not toil nor do they spin, yet I say to you that not even Solomon in all his glory clothed himself like one of these. But if God so clothes the grass of the field, which is alive today and tomorrow is thrown into the furnace, will He not much more clothe you? You of little faith!" Matthew 6:25-30 (also Philippians 4:19)

That's just creation. Man has been granted dominion for relationships in at least three other areas. These include the family, being a people, and governing ourselves, areas where man is to exercise love, caring, and sharing with others. The argument for dominion in relationships is rooted in two ideas. First, as creator, God is creation's ruler, including governance over man. *God owns all creation.* He governed His people when Moses led the Israelites out of Egypt. However, man soon rejected God's rule.

- Then all the elders of Israel gathered together and came to Samuel at Ramah; and they said to him, "Behold, you have grown old, and your sons do not walk in your ways. Now appoint a king for us to judge us like all the nations." But the thing was displeasing in the sight of Samuel when they said, "Give us a king to judge us." And Samuel prayed to the Lord. The Lord said to Samuel, "Listen to the voice of the people in regard to all that they say to you, for they have not rejected you, but they have rejected Me from being king over them. Like all the deeds which they have done since the day that I brought them up from Egypt even to this day—in that they have forsaken Me and served other gods—so they are doing to you also. Now then, listen to their voice; however, you shall solemnly warn them and tell them of the procedure of the king who will reign over them." 1 Samuel 8:5-9

When man rejected God's rule, man was left to rule himself. While God gave man dominion in these relationships, He also instituted requirements for man to follow. These requirements have their basis in passages such as the following:

- So then do not be foolish, but understand what the will of the Lord is. And do not get drunk with wine, for that is dissipation, but be filled with the Spirit, speaking to one another in psalms and hymns and spiritual songs, singing and making melody with your heart to the Lord; always giving thanks for all things in the name of our Lord Jesus Christ to God, even the Father; and be subject to one another in the fear of Christ. Ephesians 5:17-21

- [A]nd walk in love, just as Christ also loved you and gave Himself up for us, an offering and a sacrifice to God as a fragrant aroma. Ephesians 5:2

Second, God's will for man is that he voluntarily obey God, do good, and be subject to one another in love. There are two ways in which man is a part of creation. The first way was just mentioned and is voluntary on our part: our obedience to God's will. As to the second, we have no choice. We ourselves are a part of creation; we too belong to God. We therefore have a duty to care both for ourselves and others. *For this we are accountable whether we choose to accept it or not.* Each of the relationships mentioned above is grounded in the aforementioned ideas, and have their basis in man's nature (Chapter 2). They are diagramed on the following page.

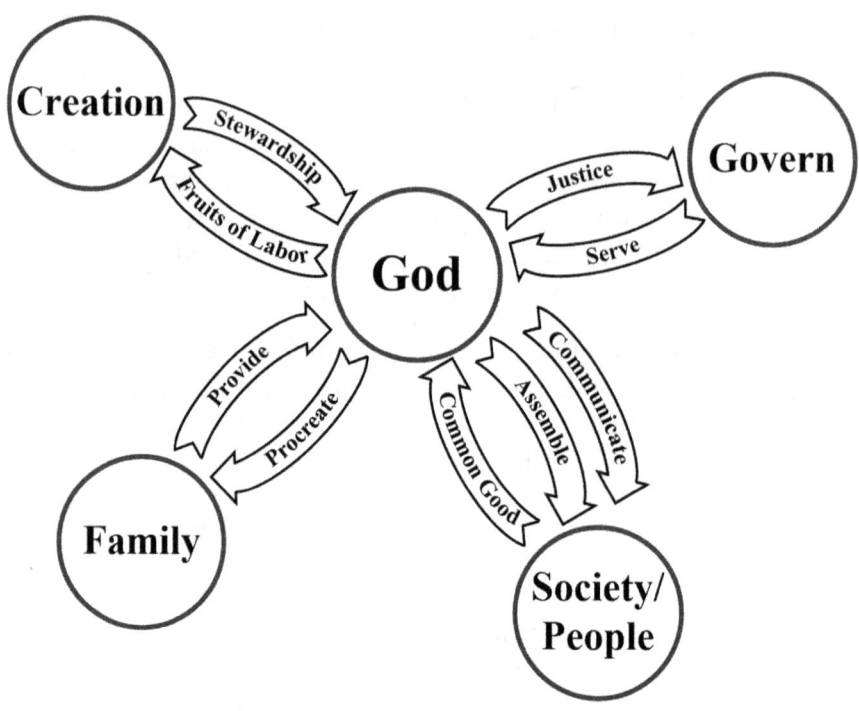

Creation

The following passages reiterate the points made earlier that God made creation, rules His creation, and granted man dominion over what He made. These are followed by passages regarding our right to keep the fruits of our labor and our corresponding duty of stewardship. Stewardship too is a form of providing for others. It can be thought of as charity across time. The decisions each generation makes impacts every future generation's ability to provide for themselves and those who come after them. While we are to enjoy what we produce, we are not to become attached to the material things we produce. Instead, as we saw in the last chapter, we are to share what we have with others in need. While these passages deal with material things we are also required to share the spiritual things, as noted in the previous chapter.

- For every beast of the forest is Mine, / The cattle on a thousand hills. / I know every bird of the mountains, / And everything that moves in the field is Mine. / If I were hungry I would not tell you, / For the world is Mine, and all it contains. Psalm 50:10-2 (also Psalm 24:1)

- For the Lord is a great God / And a great King above all gods, / In whose hand are the depths of the earth, / The peaks of the mountains are His also. / The sea is His, for it was He who made it, / And His hands formed the dry land. Psalm 95:3-5

- Then God said, "Behold, I have given you every plant yielding seed that is on the surface of all the earth, and every tree which has fruit yielding seed; it shall be food for you; and to every beast of the earth and to every bird of the sky and to every thing that moves on the earth which has life, I have given every green plant for food"; and it was so. Genesis 1:29-30

Our Right to Keep Fruits of Our Labor ...

- So then neither the one who plants nor the one who waters is anything, but God who causes the growth. Now he who plants and he who waters are one; but each will receive his own reward according to his own labor. For we are God's fellow workers; you are God's field, God's building. 1 Corinthians 3:7-9

- There is nothing better for a man than to eat and drink and tell himself that his labor is good. This also I have seen that it is from the hand of God. For who can eat and who can have enjoyment without Him? Ecclesiastes 2:24-5

- Here is what I have seen to be good and fitting: to eat, to drink and enjoy oneself in all one's labor in which he toils under the sun during the few years of his life which God has given him; for this is his reward. Furthermore, as for every man to whom God has given riches and wealth, He has also empowered him to eat from them and to receive his reward and rejoice in his labor; this is the gift of God. For he will not often consider the years of his life, because God keeps him occupied with the gladness of his heart. Ecclesiastes 5:18-20

- Thus I hated all the fruit of my labor for which I had labored under the sun, for I must leave it to the man who will come after me. And who knows whether he will be a wise man or a fool? Yet he will have control over all the fruit of my labor for which I have labored by acting wisely under the sun. This too is vanity. Ecclesiastes 2:18-9

... And Duty of Stewardship

- Then the Lord God took the man and put him into the garden of Eden to cultivate it and keep it. Genesis 2:15

- But one has testified somewhere, saying, "What is man, that You remember him? Or the son of man, that You are concerned about him? You have made him for a little while lower than the angels; You have crowned him with glory and honor, and have appointed him over the works of Your hands; You have put all things in subjection under his feet." For in subjecting all things to him, He left nothing that is not subject to him. But now we do not yet see all things subjected to him. Hebrews 2:6-8

- Above all, keep fervent in your love for one another, because love covers a multitude of sins. Be hospitable to one another without complaint. As each one has received a special gift, employ it in serving one another as good stewards of the manifold grace of God.1 Peter 4:8-10

Man was given dominion over creation to support his existence and purpose, but he is to exercise care in its use. He is therefore to use what he needs and help others as he has means. Wealth itself is not bad, but what we choose to do with it makes all the difference. We have no control over the fruits of our labor once we are gone. Those things pass to someone else.

Family

The family is one of the earliest relationships where man was given dominion. As context, I'm going to again provide a little Christian doctrine for those who do not know it so that the following can be understood in its full context. Adam was created on the sixth day of creation. Eve was created from Adam as noted in one of the next passages. Thus all man is derived from one man; we all share the same kinship. Adam and Eve's actions in the Garden of Eden resulted in man's separation from his original relationship with God. It is through Christ's sacrifice (the second Adam) that man's original relationship with God was restored. This is what is meant by a new covenant. However, this new covenant did not replace the Old Testament covenant of the Law, but fulfilled it.

Second point. We mentioned the Trinity in the first chapter. God is one and many at the same time, but not in the same sense. There are three persons within one essence or nature, and there is love between the persons within God, for God is love. Man was given God's image, an inward image, our ability to reason and know Him. While it is admittedly a very dim image, there is nothing else in all of creation closer.

The relationship that man and woman are to have is similar to the love between the three persons of the Trinity. We are commanded by God to become of one flesh when we join together in marriage. While we remain two persons, we are to become one with each other through our love for each other—each serving the other to help provide what they need. This too is a very dim image of the love God has, but there is also nothing else in all creation that is closer either.

As man is finite, he must have children to continue effectively exercising the dominion he was given, but stewardship requires education as man is not born with knowledge. Knowledge can only be acquired through our own effort. It is the parents' responsibility to instruct their children (see Chapter 3), including what is required to both effectively exercise the dominion God has given us and fulfill our duty of stewardship over that dominion. We are to use with care to be effective stewards. Otherwise we care without using, or use without caring. Neither of these latter alternatives fulfills our responsibilities. *It is not just about the outcome, but the means used to fulfill it.*

Below are a few general passages regarding man, woman, and family. These build on the foundation presented in the last two chapters on our being and actions. They are followed by passages related to our right to procreate, and the duty we have to provide as individuals. This duty applies first and foremost to those in our families. The education mentioned above is one way we are to provide. We are also to provide the material things and love needed for our children to grow into healthy citizens capable of fulfilling their purpose. But before we can educate another, we must first know and understand ourselves.

The model relating God, faith, freedom, virtue, charity, and love presented in the first chapter is always only one generation away from being lost. *It is our responsibility to provide what is needed to the next generation so that does not happen. It is the next generation's choice whether or not they will accept that duty*, and from that choice, whether they receive the benefit from the rights that only comes with acceptance.

- The man gave names to all the cattle, and to the birds of the sky, and to every beast of the field, but for Adam there was not found a helper suitable for him. So the Lord God caused a deep sleep to fall upon the man, and he slept; then He took one of his ribs and closed up the flesh at that place. The Lord God fashioned into a woman the rib which He had taken from the man, and brought her to the man. The man said, "This is now bone of my bones, and flesh of my flesh; she shall be called Woman, because she was taken out of Man." For this reason a man shall leave his father and his mother, and be joined to his wife; and they shall become one flesh. Genesis 2:20-4 (also Genesis 2:18)

- Behold, children are a gift of the Lord, / The fruit of the womb is a reward. / Like arrows in the hand of a warrior, / So are the children of one's youth. / How blessed is the man whose quiver is full of them; / They will not be ashamed / When they speak with their enemies in the gate. Psalm 127:3-5

Our Right to Procreate ...

- Then God said, "Let Us make man in Our image, according to Our likeness; and let them rule over the fish of the sea and over the birds of the sky and over the cattle and over all the earth, and over every creeping thing that creeps on the earth." God created man in His own image, in the image of God He created him; male and female He created them. God blessed them; and God said to them, "Be fruitful and multiply, and fill the earth, and subdue it; and rule over the fish of the sea and over the birds of the sky and over every living thing that moves on the earth." Genesis 1:26-8

- And God blessed Noah and his sons and said to them, "Be fruitful and multiply, and fill the earth." Genesis 9:1

... And Duty to Provide

1. Making Individual Choices

- Blessed be the God and Father of our Lord Jesus Christ, the Father of mercies and God of all comfort, who comforts us in all our affliction so that we will be able to comfort those who are in any affliction with the comfort with which we ourselves are comforted by God. For just as the sufferings of Christ are ours in abundance, so also our comfort is abundant through Christ. 2 Corinthians 1:3-5

- And the congregation of those who believed were of one heart and soul; and not one of them claimed that anything belonging to him was his own, but all things were common property to them. Acts 4:32

- Woe to him who builds his house without righteousness / And his upper rooms without justice, / Who uses his neighbor's services without pay / And does not give him his wages. Jeremiah 22:13

2. For Family

- But if anyone does not provide for his own, and especially for those of his household, he has denied the faith and is worse than an unbeliever. 1 Timothy 5:8

- I was very glad to find some of your children walking in truth, just as we have received commandment to do from the Father. Now I ask you, lady, not as though I were writing to you a new commandment, but the one which we have had from the beginning, that we love one another. And this is love, that we walk according to His commandments. This is the commandment, just as you have heard from the beginning, that you should walk in it. 2 John 1:4-6

3. For Others

- But whoever has the world's goods, and sees his brother in need and closes his heart against him, how does the love of God abide in him? Little children, let us not love with word or with tongue, but in deed and truth. 1 John 3:17-8

- Now when you reap the harvest of your land, you shall not reap to the very corners of your field, nor shall you gather the gleanings of your harvest. Nor shall you glean your vineyard, nor shall you gather the fallen fruit of your vineyard; you shall leave them for the needy and for the stranger. I am the Lord your God. Leviticus 19:9-10

- Now in case a countryman of yours becomes poor and his means with regard to you falter, then you are to sustain him, like a stranger or a sojourner, that he may live with you. Do not take usurious interest from him, but revere your God, that your countryman may live with you. You shall not give him your silver at interest, nor your food for gain. Leviticus 25:35-7

We are to have children, and through our choices we are to provide for both their physical and spiritual needs. This caring accompanied by action is not limited to just our family. It includes all who cross our path who are truly in need. We are to help as we can. However, just as we saw in the last chapter, *everyone is to also use their own talents, skills, and abilities to provide for themselves. Our purpose concerns building virtue and not simply existing on the beneficence of others.*

The actions we take, whatever we ultimately choose, is not to be coerced by others. Those who gave of their possessions in the passage from Acts chose as individuals to contribute and share their goods. They were not coerced, but made their own choices based on others' needs. One significant difference between the first century and today is that most people then lived not just in poverty, but on the very edge of subsistence itself. This only increased for a time after Rome's fall. It became very difficult to tell who was truly needy as almost everyone was in dire need, until the freedom that people acquired with Rome's fall was turned to improvements in providing food, clothing, and the material goods to better live life.[1]

Compare that to today. Most of America's poor not only have the basics of food, clothing, and shelter, but the following:

1. 80% have air conditioning versus 36% in 1970;
2. 92% have a microwave;
3. Almost 75% have a car or truck, and 31% have more than two or three;
4. Almost two-thirds have cable or satellite TV;
5. Two-thirds have at least one DVD player and 70% have a VCR;
6. 50% have a personal computer and 43% have internet access;
7. 33% have a widescreen plasma or LCD TV;
8. The average poor American has more living space than the average non-poor person living in Sweden, France, or Germany.[2]

There are now over 100 different government programs providing assistance. These offer a perverse incentive to remain on them, a safety web instead of a safety net. Here is one example. A single parent with two children living in Cook County, Illinois and a job paying $15/hour for 40 hours/week could earn in 2013 over $60,000 per year in net earned income and benefits. If that person took a raise or promotion that gave them $3/hour more, their net earned income and benefits would decline to less than $40,000 per year.[3] The median household income for Illinois during this same time was only $55,769 per year.[4] After taxes, that figure is much closer to $45,000. Such programs enslave a people by making them dependent. This governance approach is contrary to our purpose.

This is a far cry from the first century described above where almost everyone lived just trying to provide for their daily needs. That is not to say that we do not have poor today, or that we are not to care for them. It's just that the poor make up a dramatically smaller percentage of America's population today than in the first century Roman Empire. This in many respects is due to the ability we have to provide for ourselves, as well as the means to do so.[5] This is the benefit of the biblical principles underlying America's foundation.

This section was about the smallest group within society, the family. The final two sections in this chapter are about society itself. The first pertains to the people itself, and the second to its governance.

The Society of God's People

This and the next section are about different aspects of society, for we are called both as individuals and to be a single people. But first a little more history is in order.[6] As just mentioned, the principles underlying America's society are grounded in those proclaimed by God to the Israelites. Within Israelite society, Moses was judge and his brother Aaron was its chief priest. There was a separation from the beginning between religious and political power.

Religious power's purpose is to teach society about what is right. We are to know God, understand how to make good choices, fulfill our purpose, and worship Him. This power is responsible for exercising judgement in relation to the things God requires of us through His revelations. Governance is needed because not all men choose to do what is good. Governing's primary purpose is to provide justice, giving each person their due. But man's justice can only deal with his actions. Only God knows the heart, and man's final judgement is God's.

There are several fundamental differences between societies based upon God's principles and those based upon man's. *Within a society based upon God's principles, God is king and society's primary purpose is to enable man to fulfill his purpose through grace by loving Him and our fellow man. Man's equal nature is to be recognized and laws are to be created that apply equally to all. Governance exists to serve the people, primarily by promoting justice.*

However, within a society based upon man's principles, each city or town had its own god, there was a human ruler and/or priest interceding on the people's behalf, and society's primary purpose was to perpetuate itself as represented by the State. The people existed to serve society itself. Some are meant to rule and others to be ruled. Man's nature is not equal as some skills and abilities benefit society more than others. Laws are to apply to the people based upon the State's needs to perpetuate itself. [7]

Both governance models are diagrammed on the next page. The biblical-principle-based and state-religion-based societies represent the two just discussed. A more modern variation of the state-religion society (the Rights of Man model) has its basis in the philosophies developed during the Renaissance and Enlightenment periods. These all in some way attempt to put religion (Church) under political authority (State). Whether it is Henry VIII and the creation of his Anglican Church, the anti-religious sentiments contained within the French Revolution's Rights of Man, or the outright renouncing of religion altogether as in Karl Marx's writings, it all comes from the same root: man turned away from God and toward himself and an inappropriate focus on the material here and now rather than the eternal.

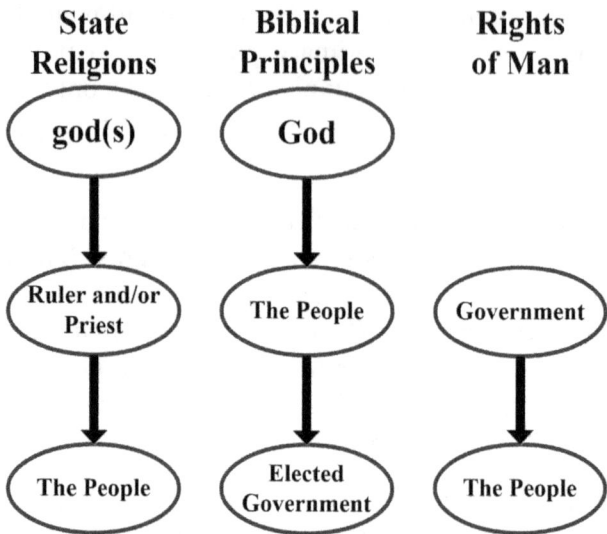

Passages related to several principles underlying the biblically-based society appear below. Throughout this discussion, we've mentioned the needs to educate so we know and then do what is good. From these requirements arise two rights and one common responsibility.

The two rights include assembly and communication. Both assembly and communication are required to educate, serve each other, and worship. In fact, they are needed to do anything successfully as a single people. The corresponding duty of supporting the common good comes from man's responsibility to choose good and not evil. However, man is to choose not based just upon his own thoughts, but God's instruction. Choices are to be grounded in morality, and morality comes only from God.

- But as for you, speak the things which are fitting for sound doctrine. Older men are to be temperate, dignified, sensible, sound in faith, in love, in perseverance. Older women likewise are to be reverent in their behavior, not malicious gossips nor enslaved to much wine, teaching what is good, so that they may encourage the young women to love their husbands, to love their children, to be sensible, pure, workers at home, kind, being subject to their own husbands, so that the word of God will not be dishonored. Likewise urge the young men to be sensible; in all things show yourself to be an example of good deeds, with purity in doctrine, dignified, sound in speech which is beyond reproach, so that the opponent will be put to shame, having nothing bad to say about us. Titus 2:1-8

- Now I exhort you, brethren, by the name of our Lord Jesus Christ, that you all agree and that there be no divisions among you, but that you be made complete in the same mind and in the same judgment. For I have been informed concerning you, my brethren, by Chloe's people, that there are quarrels among you. Now I mean this, that each one of you is saying, "I am of Paul," and "I of Apollos," and "I of Cephas," and "I of Christ." Has Christ been divided? Paul was not crucified for you, was he? Or were you baptized in the name of Paul? 1 Corinthians 1:10-3

- Come, let us worship and bow down, / Let us kneel before the Lord our Maker. / For He is our God, / And we are the people of His pasture and the sheep of His hand. / Today, if you would hear His voice, / Do not harden your hearts, as at Meribah, / As in the day of Massah in the wilderness. Psalm 95:6-8

Our Rights to Assemble ...

1. <u>To Teach</u>

    - Let the word of Christ richly dwell within you, with all wisdom teaching and admonishing one another with psalms and hymns and spiritual songs, singing with thankfulness in your hearts to God. Whatever you do in word or deed, do all in the name of the Lord Jesus, giving thanks through Him to God the Father. Colossians 3:16-7

    - What is the outcome then, brethren? When you assemble, each one has a psalm, has a teaching, has a revelation, has a tongue, has an interpretation. Let all things be done for edification. 1 Corinthians 14:26

2. To Encourage Others Through Our Actions

- [A]nd let us consider how to stimulate one another to love and good deeds, not forsaking our own assembling together, as is the habit of some, but encouraging one another; and all the more as you see the day drawing near. Hebrews 10:24-5

- Take care, brethren, that there not be in any one of you an evil, unbelieving heart that falls away from the living God. But encourage one another day after day, as long as it is still called "Today," so that none of you will be hardened by the deceitfulness of sin. Hebrews 3:12-3

3. To Sustain Fellowship and Worship

- They were continually devoting themselves to the apostles' teaching and to fellowship, to the breaking of bread and to prayer. Everyone kept feeling a sense of awe; and many wonders and signs were taking place through the apostles. And all those who had believed were together and had all things in common; and they began selling their property and possessions and were sharing them with all, as anyone might have need. Day by day continuing with one mind in the temple, and breaking bread from house to house, they were taking their meals together with gladness and sincerity of heart, praising God and having favor with all the people. And the Lord was adding to their number day by day those who were being saved. Acts 2:42-7

... And Communicate ...

1. To Encourage By Our Words

- Be kind to one another, tender-hearted, forgiving each other, just as God in Christ also has forgiven you. Ephesians 4:32

- Let your speech always be with grace, as though seasoned with salt, so that you will know how you should respond to each person. Colossians 4:6 (also Proverbs 25:11-2)

- Anxiety in a man's heart weighs it down, / But a good word makes it glad. / The righteous is a guide to his neighbor, / But the way of the wicked leads them astray. Proverbs 12:25-6

2. To Speak Truth

- Therefore, laying aside falsehood, speak truth each one of you with his neighbor, for we are members of one another. Ephesians 4:25

- The mouth of the righteous utters wisdom, / And his tongue speaks justice. / The law of his God is in his heart; / His steps do not slip. / The wicked spies upon the righteous / And seeks to kill him. Psalm 37:30-2

- For by your words you will be justified, and by your words you will be condemned. Matthew 12:37 (also Proverbs 12:17-8, 18:21)

3. To Serve One Another In Virtue

- [B]ut speaking the truth in love, we are to grow up in all aspects into Him who is the head, even Christ. Ephesians 4:15

- This you know, my beloved brethren. But everyone must be quick to hear, slow to speak and slow to anger; for the anger of man does not achieve the righteousness of God. James 1:19 (also Proverbs 18:12-3)

- But now you also, put them all aside: anger, wrath, malice, slander, and abusive speech from your mouth. Do not lie to one another, since you laid aside the old self with its evil practices. Colossians 3:8-9

... And Our Duty to Support the Common Good

1. Doing Good

- And do not neglect doing good and sharing, for with such sacrifices God is pleased. Hebrews 13:16

- Let love be without hypocrisy. Abhor what is evil; cling to what is good. Be devoted to one another in brotherly love; give preference to one another in honor; not lagging behind in diligence, fervent in spirit, serving the Lord; rejoicing in hope, persevering in tribulation, devoted to prayer, contributing to the needs of the saints, practicing hospitality. Romans 12:9-13

2. <u>In Love</u>

- By this all men will know that you are My disciples, if you have love for one another. John 13:35

- For God is not unjust so as to forget your work and the love which you have shown toward His name, in having ministered and in still ministering to the saints. And we desire that each one of you show the same diligence so as to realize the full assurance of hope until the end, so that you will not be sluggish, but imitators of those who through faith and patience inherit the promises. Hebrews 6:10-2

3. <u>And Service To One Another</u>

- For you were called to freedom, brethren; only do not turn your freedom into an opportunity for the flesh, but through love serve one another. For the whole Law is fulfilled in one word, in the statement, "You shall love your neighbor as yourself." But if you bite and devour one another, take care that you are not consumed by one another. Galatians 5:13-5

- Above all, keep fervent in your love for one another, because love covers a multitude of sins. Be hospitable to one another without complaint. As each one has received a special gift, employ it in serving one another as good stewards of the manifold grace of God. 1 Peter 4:8-10

- But now we have been released from the Law, having died to that by which we were bound, so that we serve in newness of the Spirit and not in oldness of the letter. Romans 7:6

These rights and duty concern religion's and education's roles in shaping society through the morality they are to instill. Without these moral values, society cannot be successful in the long run. But there is one more aspect of society we need to cover: governance.

Governance

The previous section stated human governing's primary responsibility is providing justice. Justice is a virtue, but it is difficult for virtue to exist in those governing if it does not already exist within the people governed. Why? Because those who rule are to come from and be elected by the people itself. People are called individually to support the common good in their interactions with each other. Providing justice supports a second side of the common good. Governance concerns making laws applying to all and executing justice when someone acts unjustly, thereby supporting the common good.

The following passages state that God is our king, but man rejected His kingship. While man was granted dominion to govern himself our rulers are to be turned toward Him. Those passages are followed by our right to justice and duty to serve society. Our right to justice is derived from two ideas. First, we each have the same nature as we were all derived from the same individual. *Therefore, we should all be treated equally in terms of our rights and duties. There should be no exceptions.* Second, we are each responsible for the choices we make. When we make bad choices, we should be held to account for them, making restitution if possible simply because *it is the right thing to do.*

Our duty to serve society is an enlargement of our duty to serve others. Some are blessed with the skills, abilities, and aptitudes necessary for governing successfully. Those who have these gifts should use them to benefit society. However, man only judges in this life. Final judgment for all rests with God alone, both for those who judge and those who are judged in this life.

- But Gideon said to them, "I will not rule over you, nor shall my son rule over you; the Lord shall rule over you." Judges 8:23

- Then all the elders of Israel gathered together and came to Samuel at Ramah; and they said to him, "Behold, you have grown old, and your sons do not walk in your ways. Now appoint a king for us to judge us like all the nations." But the thing was displeasing in the sight of Samuel when they said, "Give us a king to judge us." And Samuel prayed to the Lord. The Lord said to Samuel, "Listen to the voice of the people in regard to all that they say to you, for they have not rejected you, but they have rejected Me from being king over them. Like all the deeds which they have done since the day that I brought them up from Egypt even to this day—in that they have forsaken Me and served other gods—so they are doing to you also. Now then, listen to their voice; however, you shall solemnly warn them and tell them of the procedure of the king who will reign over them." 1 Samuel 8:5-9

- Then all the people said to Samuel, "Pray for your servants to the Lord your God, so that we may not die, for we have added to all our sins this evil by asking for ourselves a king." Samuel said to the people, "Do not fear. You have committed all this evil, yet do not turn aside from following the Lord, but serve the Lord with all your heart. You must not turn aside, for then you would go after futile things which can not profit or deliver, because they are futile." 1 Samuel 12:19-21

- The command to leave the stump of the tree with its roots means that your kingdom will be restored to you when you acknowledge that Heaven rules. Daniel 4:26

Our Right to Justice ...

1. All Authority Comes from God

- Let everyone be subject to the governing authorities, for there is no authority except that which God has established. The authorities that exist have been established by God. Consequently, whoever rebels against the authority is rebelling against what God has instituted, and those who do so will bring judgment on themselves. For rulers hold no terror for those who do right, but for those who do wrong. Do you want to be free from fear of the one in authority? Then do what is right and you will be commended. Romans 13:1-3 (NIV)

2. Rulers Are God's Servants

- For the one in authority is God's servant for your good. But if you do wrong, be afraid, for rulers do not bear the sword for no reason. They are God's servants, agents of wrath to bring punishment on the wrongdoer. Therefore, it is necessary to submit to the authorities, not only because of possible punishment but also as a matter of conscience. This is also why you pay taxes, for the authorities are God's servants, who give their full time to governing. Give to everyone what you owe them: If you owe taxes, pay taxes; if revenue, then revenue; if respect, then respect; if honor, then honor. Let no debt remain outstanding, except the continuing debt to love one another, for whoever loves others has fulfilled the law. The commandments, "You shall not commit adultery," "You shall not murder," "You shall not steal," "You shall not covet," and whatever other command there may be, are summed up in this one command: "Love your neighbor as yourself." Love does no harm to a neighbor. Therefore love is the fulfillment of the law. Romans 13:4-10 (NIV)

3. And of Good Character

- [N]amely, if any man is above reproach, the husband of one wife, having children who believe, not accused of dissipation or rebellion. For the overseer must be above reproach as God's steward, not self-willed, not quick-tempered, not addicted to wine, not pugnacious, not fond of sordid gain, but hospitable, loving what is good, sensible, just, devout, self-controlled, Titus 1:6-8

- Once the trees went forth to anoint a king over them, and they said to the olive tree, "Reign over us!" But the olive tree said to them, "Shall I leave my fatness with which God and men are honored, and go to wave over the trees?" Then the trees said to the fig tree, "You come, reign over us!" But the fig tree said to them, "Shall I leave my sweetness and my good fruit, and go to wave over the trees?" Then the trees said to the vine, "You come, reign over us!" But the vine said to them, "Shall I leave my new wine, which cheers God and men, and go to wave over the trees?" Finally all the trees said to the bramble, "You come, reign over us!" The bramble said to the trees, "If in truth you are anointing me as king over you, come and take refuge in my shade; but if not, may fire come out from the bramble and consume the cedars of Lebanon." Judges 9:8-15

- If you see oppression of the poor and denial of justice and righteousness in the province, do not be shocked at the sight; for one official watches over another official, and there are higher officials over them. After all, a king who cultivates the field is an advantage to the land. Ecclesiastes 5:8-9

4. Coming from and Elected by Their People

- [Moses said,] "Choose wise and discerning and experienced men from your tribes, and I will appoint them as your heads." You answered me and said, "The thing which you have said to do is good." So I took the heads of your tribes, wise and experienced men, and appointed them heads over you, leaders of thousands and of hundreds, of fifties and of tens, and officers for your tribes. Then I charged your judges at that time, saying, "Hear the cases between your fellow countrymen, and judge righteously between a man and his fellow countryman, or the alien who is with him. You shall not show partiality in judgment; you shall hear the small and the great alike. You shall not fear man, for the judgment is God's. The case that is too hard for you, you shall bring to me, and I will hear it." Deuteronomy 1:13-7 (also 16:18-20, Exodus 18:19-23, Numbers 11:16-7)

5. <u>Executing Impartial Justice</u>

- The strength of the King loves justice; / You have established equity; / You have executed justice and righteousness in Jacob. / Exalt the Lord our God / And worship at His footstool; / Holy is He. Psalm 99:4-5

- You shall do no injustice in judgment; you shall not be partial to the poor nor defer to the great, but you are to judge your neighbor fairly. You shall not go about as a slanderer among your people, and you are not to act against the life of your neighbor; I am the Lord. Leviticus 19:15-6

- This is what the Lord Almighty said: "Administer true justice; show mercy and compassion to one another. Do not oppress the widow or the fatherless, the foreigner or the poor. Do not plot evil against each other." Zechariah 7:9-10

6. <u>Supporting the Common Good</u>

- Woe to those who enact evil statutes / And to those who constantly record unjust decisions, / So as to deprive the needy of justice / And rob the poor of My people of their rights, / So that widows may be their spoil / And that they may plunder the orphans. Isaiah 10:1-2

- Woe to those who call evil good, and good evil; / Who substitute darkness for light and light for darkness; / Who substitute bitter for sweet and sweet for bitter! / Woe to those who are wise in their own eyes / And clever in their own sight! / Woe to those who are heroes in drinking wine / And valiant men in mixing strong drink, / Who justify the wicked for a bribe, / And take away the rights of the ones who are in the right! Isaiah 5:20-3

7. <u>But the Final Judgement is God's</u>

- Therefore you have no excuse, everyone of you who passes judgment, for in that which you judge another, you condemn yourself; for you who judge practice the same things. And we know that the judgment of God rightly falls upon those who practice such things. But do you suppose this, O man, when you pass judgment on those who practice such things and do the same yourself, that you will escape the judgment of God? Or do you think lightly of the riches of His kindness and tolerance and patience, not knowing that the kindness of God leads you to repentance? But because of your stubbornness and unrepentant heart you are storing up wrath for yourself in the day of wrath and revelation of the righteous judgment of God, who will render to each person according to his deeds: to those who by perseverance in doing good seek for glory and honor and immortality, eternal life; but to those who are selfishly ambitious and do not obey the truth, but obey unrighteousness, wrath and indignation. There will be tribulation and distress for every soul of man who does evil, of the Jew first and also of the Greek, but glory and honor and peace to everyone who does good, to the Jew first and also to the Greek. For there is no partiality with God. Romans 2:1-11

- "Why should I pardon you? / Your sons have forsaken Me / And sworn by those who are not gods. / When I had fed them to the full, / They committed adultery / And trooped to the harlot's house. / They were well-fed lusty horses, / Each one neighing after his neighbor's wife. / Shall I not punish these people," declares the Lord, / "And on a nation such as this / Shall I not avenge Myself?" Jeremiah 5:7-9 (also Isaiah 3:13-5 and 13:11)

... And Duty to Serve

1. <u>We All Serve God</u>

- Do not be called leaders; for One is your Leader, that is, Christ. But the greatest among you shall be your servant. Whoever exalts himself shall be humbled; and whoever humbles himself shall be exalted. Matthew 23:10-2

- But Jesus called them to Himself and said, "You know that the rulers of the Gentiles lord it over them, and their great men exercise authority over them. It is not this way among you, but whoever wishes to become great among you shall be your servant, and whoever wishes to be first among you shall be your slave; just as the Son of Man did not come to be served, but to serve, and to give His life a ransom for many." Matthew 20:25-8 (also Mark 10:42-5)

2. Obey Your Ruler(s)

- Remind them to be subject to rulers, to authorities, to be obedient, to be ready for every good deed, to malign no one, to be peaceable, gentle, showing every consideration for all men. For we also once were foolish ourselves, disobedient, deceived, enslaved to various lusts and pleasures, spending our life in malice and envy, hateful, hating one another. Titus 3:1-3

- Obey your leaders and submit to them, for they keep watch over your souls as those who will give an account. Let them do this with joy and not with grief, for this would be unprofitable for you. Hebrews 13:17

3. Serve While Executing Justice

- You shall not hate your fellow countryman in your heart; you may surely reprove your neighbor, but shall not incur sin because of him. You shall not take vengeance, nor bear any grudge against the sons of your people, but you shall love your neighbor as yourself; I am the Lord. Leviticus 19:17-8

Man is called to love each other in service, and this is especially true for those who would be our leaders. We are all called to obey God, including our leaders. The one who would lead is called to be the servant of all. This type of service requires some special characteristics. These include the virtues of honor and fortitude; stability in firmness; fidelity; and piety in the exercise of authority.

They should possess "strict integrity and righteousness, firm and immovable in the execution of justice and judgment."[8] They create an environment where we as individuals have the ability to exercise our rights and fulfill our responsibilities.

This environment has other attributes. Its promotion of virtue brings unity, strength, and stability to a people. This environment makes true progress possible. Virtue's absence leads to promoting self-interest, division, weakness, and instability. Those governing in the latter environment tend to look out for their own interests at the expense of those they are to serve.

The two spheres of religious and political power are to be both separate and equal within a society based on biblical principles. Both are to be oriented to God, the source of all legitimate power. Leaders in both spheres have a moral duty to serve society. They each support the common good, but do so in different ways. The primary purpose of religious power is to educate regarding God's requirements for us as His people, especially in the areas of relationship, purpose, and worship. Political power is to promote justice through the statutes it creates and their enforcement when man chooses to do wrong. Government statutes are to apply to everyone equally and be consistent with God's requirements for us, its actions are to support fulfilling our purpose.

These qualities are the very opposite of man's governance without God, and that is where we go to end this work.

Chapter 5
Implications of Human Rights

We've studied the implications our being, actions, and dominion have in shaping the natural rights we've received from God and their corresponding duties. Along the way, we discussed such topics as man's nature and purpose, morality's basis, the need for virtue within society, and human governance models.

The biblical principles inherent in these natural rights are incorporated into America's founding, and as seen in the previous chapter, they result in a radically different governance model than those based upon pagan thought. The differences between biblical and pagan principles goes to the heart of what we've discussed in the last three chapters: why the basis for our rights matters. The biblical- and pagan-based governance models, along with their underlying principles, are both contradictory and incompatible. They cannot coexist.

This chapter examines some additional differences in biblical and pagan thought. It matters. We see the resulting conflict between these two sets of principles playing out within America today, and I don't believe a significant part of our society sees the differences let alone understands it. Without knowledge, we cannot successfully keep the gifts we've been given, let alone pass them on.

There are several areas we still need to explore before a solution can be outlined. A solution does exist—if we want it. It is an answer that is both easy and difficult, like anything else that truly matters. It all comes down to the choices we are willing to make. But first we need to extend our governance discussion by further examining the separation of powers. We'll next present some implications from the differences between man's and God's values, before closing with the related topic of liberation theology.

Separation of Powers

The last chapter closed with the role and purpose of human governance, including a biblical-based principle that the spheres of religious and political power were to be separate. Further, this structure was accepted by the Israelites beginning from the time Moses led them out of Egypt. Why does this matter? To answer, we need to first define a couple more terms: religion and ideology. Within Western culture, religion is concerned with the relationship between man and some supreme being, nature, essence, or will. *Religion is a relationship beginning on Earth and extending into the Heavens.* Ideology, on the other hand, is concerned with how man interacts with others within society, particularly how he governs himself. *Ideology concerns man's relationships that begin and end on the Earth.* Religion concerns the eternal and ideology the material.

Christian principles point to religion lying within the realm of the Church and human governance within the State. Certainly, human governance existed before the Israelites left Egypt. For the Israelites, Aaron was chief priest and Moses judge. Religious power's purpose was education and conducting worship. The judge was to provide impartial justice as God was king. God's rule was supreme. But man rejected God's governance, just as man rejected his obedience to God in the Garden of Eden. While God granted man dominion in governing himself, He also directed man to love Him and our fellow man, and implement justice equally. *Love is the end; virtue the means.*

Religious and political power are not separate in the two pagan governance models. Within the state-religion-society model, religious and political power were not the same, but were very closely related. At times the ruler and priest were related, or even the same person. Sometimes the rulers (such as Egypt's pharaohs and Rome's emperors) were considered to be gods themselves. This relationship was further emphasized by placing the palace and temple close to each other, usually someplace where the entire town could see them, like a hill. Over time, these sites grew taller because the spot on which the temple was located was sacred. Whenever a new temple was needed, it was built on the ruins of the previous building.

Within societies modeled on the rights of man, there is also a close relationship between religious and political power. The only difference is that religious power, if it exists at all, lies within political power. Within this model, religious power is to be subservient to political power. This relationship aligns with the modern philosophy underlying all today's "isms": communism, fascism, progressivism, socialism, etc. These too represent a pagan notion. The state is the supreme power on earth, as there cannot be two masters. This is a corruption of the Christian model. *Yes, there cannot be two supreme powers on the Earth, because there can be no supreme power on the Earth. There is only one supreme power, and that is God.* All legitimate power derives from Him and is to be oriented toward Him.

The differences in these relationships are presented below, but. they are not derived from the governance models shown earlier. Rather man's notions about the relationship between these two powers drive the form of governance model he uses. In only one instance, the model built upon Christian principles, do religious and political power have the chance to play their proper biblical role within society. All other models have their basis in pagan thought and result in the eventual corruption of both religious and political power. The difference in these relationships is fundamental in supporting our natural rights that in turn support fulfilling our purpose. It is these biblical principles America was founded upon.

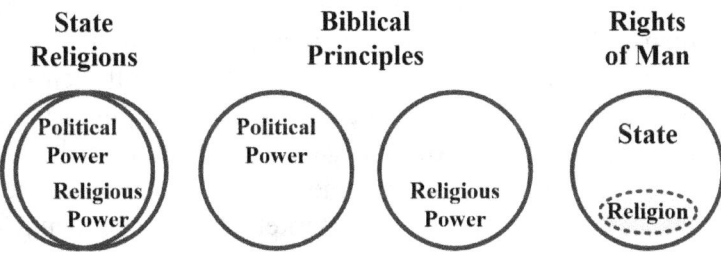

Man's Virtue and God's

We can extend this discussion of pagan thought further. We've mentioned many times in this book the need for virtue, righteousness, and doing good. Without that underlying morality, a people cannot be successful in the long run. Here's another difference. Within pagan philosophy, virtue is a balance, a blending of virtue and vice, a mixing of white and black into grey. Actions are a mixture of both virtue and vice, of good and evil. Man is to try and become, on balance, more virtuous than controlled by vice.

Christian principles stand this notion on its head. Within Christian thought, there is only virtue and only vice. Each are derived from different sources: virtue from good and vice from evil. Evil is the absence of good. You can only choose one or the other. There is no balance, no blending. There is only black and only white, both fully present at the same time. One can choose only one or the other. The two approaches cannot coexist, just like the biblical and pagan notions of political and religious power, or differences in the related governance models based on those notions.

But actions alone are not enough. We are called to both know and do. The motive for our actions is to be love—agape. We are to serve others and thereby fulfill our purpose. This service can be to anyone: our parents, spouse, family, friends, co-workers, or a total stranger. Performing actions without love is the Pharisee's hypocrisy:

- Then Jesus spoke to the crowds and to His disciples, saying: "The scribes and the Pharisees have seated themselves in the chair of Moses; therefore all that they tell you, do and observe, but do not do according to their deeds; for they say things and do not do them. They tie up heavy burdens and lay them on men's shoulders, but they themselves are unwilling to move them with so much as a finger. But they do all their deeds to be noticed by men; for they broaden their phylacteries and lengthen the tassels of their garments. They love the place of honor at banquets and the chief seats in the synagogues, and respectful greetings in the market places, and being called

Rabbi by men. But do not be called Rabbi; for One is your Teacher, and you are all brothers. Do not call anyone on earth your father; for One is your Father, He who is in heaven. Do not be called leaders; for One is your Leader, that is, Christ. But the greatest among you shall be your servant. Whoever exalts himself shall be humbled; and whoever humbles himself shall be exalted." Matthew 23:1-12

The Pharisees used words without value; they performed actions without love. They were self-serving instead of self-sacrificing. They held moral values rooted in the pagan notion that actions alone matter, and that on balance those actions just needed to be more good than evil instead of actions rooted in love. These are the false choices of 'the lesser evil' often presented to us today by leaders who exempt themselves from the very laws they create. A do as I say and not as I do governance approach.

Without love, our actions are meaningless. Man's morality is insufficient as his basis is insufficient; man is not inherently good as God is good. It is because of God's nature that His morality has value. But are there other implications in using man's morality? Does morality's basis really matter? That is where we must head next.

Man's Morality

America was founded on biblically-based principles, not the Bible or Christianity itself. This morality, both the values and principles derived from it, provided the societal foundation for our governing structures. Over the last fifty years or so, we've seen a dramatic shift in our society's acceptance of Christianity and therefore those underlying principles. We've gone from active support, to ambivalence, to tolerance, to active opposition today. As a country, we are moving away from many of our founding principles, those our societal structures rest upon. It shouldn't be surprising there is conflict as those principles are contrary to the pagan ones being trotted out today. Christianity is a threat to this shift that must be eliminated. As noted above, the two world views are both contrary and incompatible.

Some in our society are turned from God toward man for their morality and values, and are deriving their principles from that choice. There are several implications of this shift that must be considered as both individuals and a society.

First, man has not entirely rejected God's values. Instead, he picks and chooses which values to keep and which to reject. He keeps equality, but one based upon outcomes (the material) instead of our nature (the eternal). He keeps charity, but one based upon government assistance (dependence) instead of individual self-sacrifice in assisting others (independence). He keeps tolerance, but only if you agree with his values. Done away with are values such as the sanctity of life (abortion and euthanasia), marriage (same sex marriage), and differences in gender (bathroom bills, for example). They've become empty actions, words without love, just as with the Pharisees.

Second, can man just pick and choose which of God's values and morality to keep? No. I've already stated that man's nature is itself insufficient to create his own values and for them to have any meaning. But there is another reason. For man to be independent of God's morality, he must reject all of it. If man accepts any part, no matter how small, then he is still subject to God's morality, a morality based upon God's nature and authority alone.

Third, if man does create and accept his own values, then his God-given equality of nature is no longer recognized. You see, if man makes his own values, then someone must decide what those values are and others must be the ones to follow them. This is the same pagan notion that some are meant to rule and others to be ruled. In the words of Plato and other Greek philosophers, this is both right and just. One group will view themselves as the elite, and the other those needing direction to live worthwhile lives, with worthwhile being defined by the elite. Over time each group will grow to resent the other. The love we are to have for each other will not be present as it should. Just look at the divisions present today within our society, churches, and political powers. *Division is the fruit of man turned from God.*

Fourth, man's picking and choosing his own values leads to their loss of content, a form of nominalism. The words representing values become labels without meaning. The values within God's morality have content, because their meaning have their basis in Him. There is no good or bad anymore with man's values. There are no objective values for his reason to use in determining what is right or wrong. Instead, man is left with his emotions to determine his values, and those emotions will lead man to what he wants at the moment. You can't have it both ways. To believe so is to lie to oneself.

Fifth, if we turn from God's values, then the nature He gave man will no longer be recognized. Because man loses his humanity. He becomes no different from the rest of creation. Man's reason no longer has its God-given basis or purpose. There is no longer faith, and without faith there can be no hope or charity. Without these, there can be no virtue. Man will have conquered all of nature, only to lose everything—including himself.

This is all fine in theory, but let me provide an example in support of the points made above. Let's take marriage. According to biblical principles, marriage is a relationship where a man and woman join themselves to one another, becoming of one flesh. The biblical value is that marriage is between one man and one woman. Man wishes to change the value of marriage to be between two consenting people, regardless of their sex. But why that value? Why not marriage between more than two people? If someone wants, then shouldn't they be allowed to marry anyone, regardless of their age, be they a child, elderly, or infirm? Why should it matter whether they are related or not? Finally, why should marriage be limited to only being between people? What makes any one of these values better than any other? What standard can man point to that provides an objective basis for his choice? The truth is, there isn't any. Man becomes driven by emotions, what he wants.

When cut loose from God's morality, marriage becomes a value empty of content. It becomes merely a label. Can we assume that all men want the same things from life once he has created his own set of values? There is no evidence that is the case. After all, if this were true we'd likely want only one type of house, one style of clothing, or one kind of bread.

But there is plenty of evidence that in societies driven by pagan notions, choices become very limited, at least for those not a part of the self-proclaimed elite. Housing projects become the norm. One basic car is produced for those who can afford it. There is little innovation. There are shortages of food and other consumer products. This must be the case. Why? Because millions of people make hundreds of millions of independent decisions based upon the principles and values they hold. No one can devise a system capable of accounting for all of those differences. Only man turned toward himself is arrogant enough to believe he can do so by simply reducing the number of choices.

Not only are our wants generally different, but in many cases, they are not consistent over time either. I guess we can chalk this up to justice. Man, in trying to set himself up as God, commits rebellion and suffers spiritual death. But it doesn't have to be that way. It all comes back again to our choices.

God's values are timeless. They are anchored in His truth and goodness, qualities that exist outside of time. His standards are objective as they lie outside of man, but not outside of man's abilities—with God's help. Man is not bad; he is just not up to the task on his own, and maybe that is part of the lesson we are to learn in this life.

Man is insufficient as a starting point for such a task as creating his own values as he is both finite and not inherently good. Not all humans like the same thing, to the same degree, in the same proportion or manner. These make it impossible for man to create meaningful values on his own.

There is one final area to look at before we talk about the answer. So far we've looked at the separation between religious and political power, and how those powers are promulgated through virtue. This section largely focused on some implications for political power. The next section turns to religious power.

Liberation Theology

With the rising rejection of Christian thought and principles, there came along something called *liberation theology* about fifty or sixty years ago. While attributed to the Latin American Catholic Church, it is not limited to that part of the world or denomination. We've also seen similar corrosive ideas take root in the so-called interfaith movement.[1] Both represent corruption of the Christian principles laid out in earlier chapters, a pagan corruption that affects our natural rights. Liberation theology selectively uses the Bible to pick and choose which of God's values it accepts, thereby rejecting others. This is no different from the Marcion heresy outlined in Chapter 1.

It is simply another application of the rights of man model. Not like communism as liberation theology is not atheistic, and not like fascism or Henry VIII's Anglican Church, where the church was under more direct government control. Instead, it is more like the thoughts expressed by Baruch Spinoza, removing God's duality, thereby changing biblical principles to effectively remove God's influence from Christianity. One way Spinoza did this was to remove the separation between creator and creation. If nature and creator are one, then human actions become displays of His action and not doctrine. This gives man control over religion, and fits with socialist and progressive notions which seek to keep some moral basis to exercise control, but making it man's morality. More about this idea appears later in the chapter.

What is liberation theology? At its core, liberation theology promotes freedom for all who are oppressed and the elimination of poverty, with actions to bring those about being actively taken by society. Sounds okay, doesn't it? However, it's not just individuals who are to use their power in support of these goals, but all of society's structures are to also use their power—including the church and state. Some passages it relies on to support its beliefs include the following.

Freedom for the Oppressed

- The Spirit of the Lord God is upon me, / Because the Lord has anointed me / To bring good news to the afflicted; / He has sent me to bind up the brokenhearted, / To proclaim liberty to captives. / And freedom to prisoners. Isaiah 61:1

The Elimination of Poverty

- At the end of every seven years you must cancel debts. This is how it is to be done: Every creditor shall cancel any loan they have made to a fellow Israelite. They shall not require payment from anyone among their own people, because the Lord's time for canceling debts has been proclaimed. You may require payment from a foreigner, but you must cancel any debt your fellow Israelite owes you. However, there need be no poor people among you, for in the land the Lord your God is giving you to possess as your inheritance, he will richly bless you, if only you fully obey the Lord your God and are careful to follow all these commands I am giving you today. Deuteronomy 15:1-5

- On this year of jubilee each of you shall return to his own property. If you make a sale, moreover, to your friend or buy from your friend's hand, you shall not wrong one another. Corresponding to the number of years after the jubilee, you shall buy from your friend; he is to sell to you according to the number of years of crops. In proportion to the extent of the years you shall increase its price, and in proportion to the fewness of the years you shall diminish its price, for it is a number of crops he is selling to you. Leviticus 25:13-6

- For there was not a needy person among them, for all who were owners of land or houses would sell them and bring the proceeds of the sales and lay them at the apostles' feet, and they would be distributed to each as any had need. Acts 4:34-5 (also Acts 2:44-5)

- For this is not for the ease of others and for your affliction, but by way of equality—at this present time your abundance being a supply for their need, so that their abundance also may become a supply for your need, that there may be equality; as it is written, "He who gathered much did not have too much, and he who gathered little had no lack." 2 Corinthians 8:13-4

Man Must Take Action to Correct Moral Wrongs

- Do not think that I came to bring peace on the earth; I did not come to bring peace, but a sword. For I came to set a man against his father, and a daughter against her mother, and a daughter-in-law against her mother-in-law; and a man's enemies will be the members of his household. Matthew 10:34-6

- He has done mighty deeds with His arm; He has scattered those who were proud in the thoughts of their heart. He has brought down rulers from their thrones, And has exalted those who were humble. He has filled the hungry with good things; And sent away the rich empty-handed. Luke 1:51-3

- And He said to them, "When I sent you out without money belt and bag and sandals, you did not lack anything, did you?" They said, "No, nothing." And He said to them, "But now, whoever has a money belt is to take it along, likewise also a bag, and whoever has no sword is to sell his coat and buy one. For I tell you that this which is written must be fulfilled in Me, 'And He was numbered with transgressors'; for that which refers to Me has its fulfillment." They said, "Lord, look, here are two swords." And He said to them, "It is enough." Luke 22:35-8

This theology views the world from the poor's perspective. It claims to promote justice, and one can find several types of justice it supports, including economic, environmental, ethnic, gender, racial, and social, just to name a few. Encompassed within these justices are a different view of man's being and dominion. There is a call to action to correct what this worldview sees as injustice. Make no mistake, no one should want poverty, discrimination, pollution, or any type of injustice. But within liberation theology, it is all about the ends to be achieved, and not the means.

And therein lies the rub. As we've seen repeatedly, the means do matter. If the right means are not used, then the ends themselves are empty. Just like the actions of the Pharisees. As already mentioned, liberation theology's thoughts have their basis in the same heresies discussed in Chapter 1, and just like some originators of those heresies, some were pious people who intended to save Christianity from itself.

Liberation theology says its end must be achieved—now—by whatever means necessary. Underlying this idea is the thought God is inadequate, that God must therefore rely on man, or man rely on himself. Another heresy. Further, that Jesus came with a sword as liberator of the oppressed, not a peacemaker who acted through love. They are claiming some special knowledge for the parts of the Bible they choose to support their thought, while ignoring others that contradict it—a form of gnosticism. Much of what I've read states that liberation theology incorporates Marxism into its doctrine, but it is more basic than that: They incorporate pagan thought that is not based upon God's direction for us; instead it is based upon man's self-direction.

Social institutions are to be used to correct today's imbalances. This ignores one of the most significant portions of the New Testament, the Sermon on the Mount. Jesus did not go to the Sanhedrin in Jerusalem to give this sermon to the religious leaders, nor did he go to Pilate or his advisors to give them to Rome's governing power. Instead, He gave these teachings to those individuals who came to hear him. *He spoke about what they should know and do in caring for others, whether they are poor in spirit or material possessions. Liberation theology places the material world over the spiritual, the idea that by bringing about the ends, the means will follow. It is an empty notion, because it is based upon man's values and not God's.*

But, can the assertions presented in the last paragraph be supported? I think so by looking at what we are to know and do: our purpose, actions, and their fruit. The virtue of justice is simply each person receiving their due, and what they are due is based upon their choices and actions. How are we to choose? What are our actions to be?

The answers to these questions goes back to the principles underlying our natural rights and duties outlined in the last three chapters. We are to put spiritual things above the material; the things of this life only support our existence in fulfilling our purpose. We are to be impartial in enacting justice, recognizing the equality of man's nature. We are to use God's gift of freedom in choosing and doing good, and serving one another, out of love for God and each other. When man fails in the task at hand, we should be asking why it occurred, and not use it as an excuse to pull away from God and turn toward ourselves. God is not the source of our failure, the failure rests with man.

What Are We to Know and Do?

1. Choose the Spiritual Over the Material

- But just as you abound in everything, in faith and utterance and knowledge and in all earnestness and in the love we inspired in you, see that you abound in this gracious work also. I am not speaking this as a command, but as proving through the earnestness of others the sincerity of your love also. For you know the grace of our Lord Jesus Christ, that though He was rich, yet for your sake He became poor, so that you through His poverty might become rich. 2 Corinthians 8:7-9

- Do not store up for yourselves treasures on earth, where moth and rust destroy, and where thieves break in and steal. But store up for yourselves treasures in heaven, where neither moth nor rust destroys, and where thieves do not break in or steal; for where your treasure is, there your heart will be also. Matthew 6: 19-21

- Listen, my beloved brethren: did not God choose the poor of this world to be rich in faith and heirs of the kingdom which He promised to those who love Him? But you have dishonored the poor man. Is it not the rich who oppress you and personally drag you into court? James 2:5-6

2. Enact Justice Impartially

- You shall do no injustice in judgment; you shall not be partial to the poor nor defer to the great, but you are to judge your neighbor fairly. Leviticus 19:15

- You shall not bear a false report; do not join your hand with a wicked man to be a malicious witness. You shall not follow the masses in doing evil, nor shall you testify in a dispute so as to turn aside after a multitude in order to pervert justice; nor shall you be partial to a poor man in his dispute. Exodus 23:1-3

- You shall not show partiality in judgment; you shall hear the small and the great alike. You shall not fear man, for the judgment is God's. The case that is too hard for you, you shall bring to me [Moses], and I will hear it. Deuteronomy 1:17

3. Use Our Freedom To Choose Good

- For such is the will of God that by doing right you may silence the ignorance of foolish men. Act as free men, and do not use your freedom as a covering for evil, but use it as bondslaves of God. Honor all people, love the brotherhood, fear God, honor the king. 1 Peter 2:15-7

- It was for freedom that Christ set us free; therefore keep standing firm and do not be subject again to a yoke of slavery. Galatians 5:1

- For you were called to freedom, brethren; only do not turn your freedom into an opportunity for the flesh, but through love serve one another. For the whole Law is fulfilled in one word, in the statement, "You shall love your neighbor as yourself." But if you bite and devour one another, take care that you are not consumed by one another. Galatians 5:13-5

- For speaking out arrogant words of vanity they entice by fleshly desires, by sensuality, those who barely escape from the ones who live in error, promising them freedom while they themselves are slaves of corruption; for by what a man is overcome, by this he is enslaved. 2 Peter 2:18-9

4. <u>Do Good To All</u>

- But love your enemies, and do good, and lend, expecting nothing in return; and your reward will be great, and you will be sons of the Most High; for He Himself is kind to ungrateful and evil men. Luke 6:35

- Do not judge, and you will not be judged; and do not condemn, and you will not be condemned; pardon, and you will be pardoned. Luke 6:37

- Beware of practicing your righteousness before men to be noticed by them; otherwise you have no reward with your Father who is in heaven. So when you give to the poor, do not sound a trumpet before you, as the hypocrites do in the synagogues and in the streets, so that they may be honored by men. Truly I say to you, they have their reward in full. But when you give to the poor, do not let your left hand know what your right hand is doing, so that your giving will be in secret; and your Father who sees what is done in secret will reward you. Matthew 6:1-4

- Jesus said to him, "If you wish to be complete, go and sell your possessions and give to the poor, and you will have treasure in heaven; and come, follow Me." But when the young man heard this statement, he went away grieving; for he was one who owned much property. Matthew 19:21-2 (also Mark 10:21-2 and Luke 18:22-3)

- But Judas Iscariot, one of His disciples, who was intending to betray Him, said, "Why was this perfume not sold for three hundred denarii and given to poor people?" Now he said this, not because he was concerned about the poor, but because he was a thief, and as he had the money box, he used to pilfer what was put into it. John 12:4-6

5. <u>Only Love Provides the Way</u>

- No one can serve two masters; for either he will hate the one and love the other, or he will be devoted to one and despise the other. You cannot serve God and wealth. Matthew 6:24

- If I have the gift of prophecy, and know all mysteries and all knowledge; and if I have all faith, so as to remove mountains, but do not have love, I am nothing. And if I give all my possessions to feed the poor, and if I surrender my body to be burned, but do not have love, it profits me nothing. Love is patient, love is kind and is not jealous; love does not brag and is not arrogant, does not act unbecomingly; it does not seek its own, is not provoked, does not take into account a wrong suffered, does not rejoice in unrighteousness, but rejoices with the truth; bears all things, believes all things, hopes all things, endures all things. 1 Corinthians 13:2-7

Charity's Fruit

We are to help others as we can, doing good by performing acts of charity. As we saw in the first chapter, charity is one of the virtues orienting man toward God, and is the action in which all other virtues end. All virtues produce charity. But what is charity? Is it just about giving? Is it simply about money or something more?

We will use the following definition for charity: *the funding or aiding of those in need in a way which builds virtue in both the giver and receiver.* This definition has several advantages. First, it doesn't confine the form of charity. Second, it doesn't specify to whom charity should be shown. Third, it doesn't limit how charity should be provided. It states that charity is between two or more people; at least one person has a need they cannot fulfill on their own, and at least one other person acts to assist them in fulfilling that need, with the sole motivation being love for the person in need, simply because they share the same nature.[2]

This definition supports the transformative nature charity is to fill in our lives. Our choices of doing good for the right reason transform us. We become good and thereby fulfill our purpose. Performing charity should create virtue in both giver and receiver, but this can only occur when both are motivated by the right reason. Charity should not lead to a person's becoming more dependent, but instead assist in creating independence, enabling a person to better care for themselves.[3] We were each created for this. And this is why charities such as Habitat for Humanity are successful. They teach the stewardship part of home ownership in addition to that created through sweat equity, so the new owner is vested with the home and the understanding to care for it.

A little earlier we defined justice as being given what one is due, what one has earned, be it good or bad. We can think of charity as being given what one is not due, what one has not earned. *It is a gift given by one person to another unconditionally out of love—grace.* Think of virtues such as forgiveness, mercy, and hospitality.

American Charity

The Charities Aid Foundation annually performs a global analysis measuring charity in three ways: monetary donations, volunteering time, and helping a stranger. Data is collected by country through research conducted as part of Gallup's World View World Poll. A country index is calculated by averaging the three measures, and a ranking is created based upon the index value. The U.S. 2010 and 2017 values are shown below.[4]

Year	Ranking	Index	Helping	Time	Donations
2010	5	55	65	39	60
2017	5	56	73	41	56

Overall, the results are pretty stable. The Foundation's approach is designed to provide information about an entire country. As such, it is not possible to determine the effects of internal differences within a country due to things such as tax policy, religious beliefs, regional attitudes towards giving, etc.

However, there is information about charitable giving within the U.S. in other sources. One such source is Albert C. Brooks' book *Who Really Cares*.[5] This source provides information on who gives, in terms of both time and money. Brook's research indicates that about 33% of the American population views itself as religious, another 27% as secular, with the remainder lying somewhere in between. Several findings include the following:

1. Those who view themselves as religious give the most, regardless of their political ideology or the religion they profess. They also not only give more to religious organizations, but secular ones as well.

2. 91% of people viewing themselves as religious give to charity compared to only 66% of those identifying themselves as secular, and on average religious people give 3.5 times more.

3. People viewing themselves as religious also donate more time than those identifying as secular, 67% to 44%. They also volunteer more frequently than those viewing themselves as secular, 12 versus 5.8 times per year.

The above all indicate that people identifying themselves as religious generally perform more charitable acts. When we cross that information with the conservative/liberal figures noted above, we get something interesting. Those figures are shown in the table below. Note the results do not sum to the figures above as not all religious or secular individuals view themselves as either conservative or liberal; some fall into that group between the two.

	Religious	Secular
Conservative	19.1%	7.3%
Liberal	6.4%	10.5%

The preceding is all about who gives. But why do Americans give? I assert that ideas matter, that they shape our thoughts and those thoughts shape our actions. It was noted earlier that those viewing themselves as religious give more than those who are secular. The table above indicates that more religious individuals view themselves as conservative whereas more secular people view themselves as liberal. I assert that those viewing themselves as religious are more likely to hold ideas consistent with a God-focused morality and virtue than those viewing themselves as secular.

There are many anecdotes in Brook's book appearing to support this notion. One such story is the following. The average South Dakotan family gives away 75% more of its household income each year than the average family in San Francisco. In interviewing an executive at the South Dakota Community Foundation about why South Dakota families donate so much to charities, she responded, "We were all taught to tithe here." She also added that even those who did not attend church were taught by their parents who likely did attend.[6] Education is one thing, *but we generally choose to act on what we learn if we believe it is the right thing to do*. Man being turned toward God matters. It shapes our ideas, which in turn shape both our actions and their motivation, as has been described in many ways within this work.

The Answer

So what's the answer? It starts with who Jesus is, what He promised, and what He's called us to do. As to who He is,

- Jesus said to him, "I am the way, and the truth, and the life; no one comes to the Father but through Me. If you had known Me, you would have known My Father also; from now on you know Him, and have seen Him." John 14:6-7

God is the only way to truth and life, and Christ is one with the Father—so His promises matter. What did He promise?

- Jesus said to her, "I am the resurrection and the life; he who believes in Me will live even if he dies, and everyone who lives and believes in Me will never die. Do you believe this?" She said to Him, "Yes, Lord; I have believed that You are the Christ, the Son of God, even He who comes into the world." John 11:25-7

We have His promise of eternal life when we voluntarily choose to give ourselves to Him. God's word is eternal, spoken one time for all time, and He cannot lie. Finally, what are we called to do? This comes from two passages.

- Let your light shine before men in such a way that they may see your good works, and glorify your Father who is in heaven. Matthew 5:16

- Whoever then annuls one of the least of these commandments, and teaches others to do the same, shall be called least in the kingdom of heaven; but whoever keeps and teaches them, he shall be called great in the kingdom of heaven. "For I say to you that unless your righteousness surpasses that of the scribes and Pharisees, you will not enter the kingdom of heaven." Matthew 5:19-20

We are to do good works aligned with the Father's will, and develop a righteous character. Righteousness is defined as the quality of being morally upright—virtuous. By obeying His will we become good.

The process we are to follow is the easy part. It creates a journey open to all. The actions we need to perform include the following:[7]

1. Turn toward God and ask for His help.
2. Learning who He is by studying and developing a personal relationship with Him.
3. Choosing to follow Him.
4. Acting on that choice through service to others.
5. Allowing ourselves to be transformed by our choices and actions, becoming good and thereby fulfilling our purpose.

These actions are relatively easy as they are all within our control. We voluntarily choose them. In terms of process, it's all about our choices.

Implications of Human Rights

This journey has both spiritual and temporal aspects, which include the following:

Spiritual Aspects

1. Prayer. Pray not just for ourselves, but our leaders, nation, and others.
2. Know your faith and your story, how Christ has made a difference in your life so you can share it when necessary.
3. Live showing Christ to others through our actions.
4. Expect accountability from others claiming to follow God by simply demanding they speak, teach, and live the truth.

Temporal Aspects

1. Educate ourselves and share what we learn with others.
2. Stand and act for what you believe. It is not about proving your faith, but defending it.
3. Engage with others: in your family, community, church, and government. Strangers too.

With these actions, we learn truth and develop wisdom. Man generally has two reactions to a crisis: fight or flight. Those are man's ways. God is asking us to choose a third way, to accept and face whatever comes our way.

- "These things I have spoken to you, so that in Me you may have peace. In the world you have tribulation, but take courage; I have overcome the world." John 16:33

This third way requires the virtue of humility, as opposed to the vice of pride. Humility is power under control, giving God the glory in service to others. Humility is not thinking less of yourself, but thinking of yourself less.[8]

Now to the more difficult part. Making the journey won't be easy because the world will resist it. But don't worry, we have help. To be successful, there are at least three things we each must hold on to.

They are God, His moral instruction, and His governance. We'll briefly look at each of these before closing.

Hold on to God, No Matter What

God is cause of all things through His creation. Such causes cannot be demonstrated, only defended. But that doesn't mean we cannot use logic to make inferences, attempting to draw some understanding from the things we do know.

1. <u>God Exists</u>

Either God exists, or He does not. If He does not exist in the first place, then how can we explain existence itself? There are theories put forth about other means for creation, but they are just that: theories searching for any support. What evidence there is supports the biblical notion of creation better than any other theory. Putting belief in other theories is irrational in the absence of evidence, belief coming from man creating his own values and also passing judgment on them.

We already briefly discussed this alternative in Chapter 1. The real question is why something exists rather than nothing. There is existence, of that there should be no doubt. If you don't believe that, then please stop by for coffee sometime. I'll pour it from above your head into a cup in your lap. After all, if I miss it won't matter. If there's no existence, then you don't exist.

If God exists, then there are at least two other possible reasons for not following Him. Either God is one with creation or He does not care about creation at all. We'll explore the faulty reasoning supporting each of these choices next.

2. <u>God is Separate from Nature</u>

All creation involves separation, not unification. If there is a house, there is a builder. If there is a work of art, there is an artist. If there is a car, there is a manufacturer. If there is a creation, there must be a creator. The real difference here is that we are not talking about creating a simple object, but all of creation. Something so vast it appears to approach infinity, if indeed it is not infinite. Only something infinite, like God, can create something from nothing, let alone something so vast.

Nothing finite (like man) has ever been able to create something from nothing. Man cannot create, he can only transform. Creation itself is not so much a final product, but rather the material from which other things can be created. Each of the examples in the preceding paragraph take raw materials and turn them into some final good useful to man.

But there is another angle to consider. Extending the analogy above, the builder must have existed before the house, the artist before the art, the manufacture before the car. There must be time, a type of order, existing in conjunction with creation.

Judeo-Christian beliefs provide the only explanation for all of the above. *There is a Creator. He is eternal and therefore outside of time. He created everything that has ever been created.*

3. Man Holds a Unique Place Within Creation

Pagan thought holds that man too is no different from creation. We can extend the last argument above to refute this idea. An elephant possesses much strength, but can it build a house? A dog is very loyal and seeks to please its master, but can it paint a picture or write a story, even a very bad one? An ape is a very intelligent animal, but can it build a car? *The answer to all these questions is no.*

Man is the only creature in all of creation who can do any of these things. Therefore, while man is a part of creation, he must at least hold a distinct place within it. Postmodernism holds the Eastern perspective that all creation is one. If this is true, then man must be no different from the rest of creation. However, we've just seen this is not the case. G. K. Chesterton provides another explanation.

> There is no equality in nature; also, there is no inequality in nature. Inequality, as much as equality, implies a standard of value. To read aristocracy into the anarchy of animals is just as sentimental as to read

democracy into it. Both aristocracy and democracy are human ideas: the one saying that all men are valuable, the other that some men are more valuable.[9]

Aristocracy and democracy are ideas unique to man. I hold that the sole difference between man and the rest of nature above is due to only one thing: man has been given God's image. I would add that some individuals' failure to recognize this is because they are applying human values, labels without content, because they are not currently turned toward God. God's image within man is very dim, but there is nothing else in all of creation that is closer. *Man is distinct, or separate if you will, from the rest of creation, just as God as creator is not one with creation. It is God's Being that provides substance to values; when man is turned toward himself those values cease to have meaning.*

4. God Loves, Therefore He Must Care

Eastern religions, ancient pagan religions, and the New Age movement accept the proposition that nature is our mother. We must worship the creator within, the creator that is also within nature. If true, we must look at our neighbor as our self. However, love is not possible if we are all one. *Love is experiential. It requires an object outside of ourselves to experience.* This is true for any love, the love to be between man and God, between man, and between man and nature. It is man's love for nature that allows for true progress to occur.

Christian beliefs assert that nature is our sister, man and nature both created by the same creator, but separate. God created all of creation out of love, nothing else. The following passage was written by Clement of Alexandria in the second century, almost two thousand years ago.

> For assuredly He does not hate anything, and yet wish that which He hates to exist. Nor does He wish anything not to exist, and yet become the cause of existence to that which he wishes not to exist. Nor does He wish anything not to exist which yet exists. If, then,

the Word hates anything, He does not wish it to exist. But nothing exists, that cause of whose existence is not supplied by God. Nothing, then, is hated by God, nor yet by the Word. For both are one – that is, God. ... If then He hates none of the things which He has made, it follows that He loves them. Much more than the rest, and with reason, will He love man, the noblest of all objects created by Him, and a God-loving being. Therefore God is loving; consequently the Word is loving.[10]

If God is one as a simple unity, then how does He have love to give? An answer lies in Christianity alone, there being a single Triune God. *A God that is personal. A God that became man.* As there are three persons within one single essence, there is community, and therefore love can exist. One can only give what they've got.

One last point. In embracing the universalist view of God and worshipping the God within, we end up worshipping ourselves. *We would worship man. This single God cannot love as there is no Being.* It must give creation something it does not possess. Chesterton points out the implications of this difference. "According to most philosophers, God in making the world enslaved it. According to Christianity, in making it, He set it free."[11]

As man, we can ask how is a Triune God possible? As finite human beings trying to understand the infinite, we can only respond it is a mystery, because *He is God.*

Hold on to His Morality, No Matter What

This whole book has been about the importance of God's moral instruction. There is not much more I can add. Just a couple additional quick examples.

We can examine suicide and martyrdom. Some free thinkers believe there is no difference between the two, whereas Christianity holds they are opposites. *The difference is love. The suicide cares so little for them self they are unwilling to live. The martyr loves another so much they are willing to die for them.* Suicide is tragic, but centers around a lack of love, even for self; it centers on self-interest. True martyrdom emphasizes self-sacrifice for another. Saying these are the same is not only foolish but irrational.

Pagan thought would assert that oil and water were a type of balance between liquids. But this is only possible if you spin them fast enough in a small enough area that they appear to come together. It requires continuous effort to deny their real nature. The more you wish them to blend, the greater the effort one must continually exert. They naturally separate when the effort stops, and that is Christianity's point. It simply acknowledges the nature of each, that each are fully present and fully different. One can draw a hippopotamus to look like a horse, but then it is no longer a hippopotamus.

A second example from the media. Most media today lacks objectivity; it paints a false picture, one that focuses on negative impressions to drive man's ideology. At times it parades human vices as virtuous. Good is evil, and evil is good. Sometimes evil is just ignored, or there are attempts to explain it away.

The media claims it's not their fault; bad news sells. But its focus also conveys the false image that everyone is doing it, and the media is only reporting what is commonplace—normal. Why would the viewer want to be left out, or not wish for government to protect them from some evil? It is man creating his own values and trying to convince others to accept and follow them. These values are contrary to God's morality because they do not promote righteousness. They are human values, empty of content.

But we shouldn't be surprised. A Pew Research survey of journalists indicate that 68 and 58 percent of national and local journalists respectively either never go to church or only go a few times a year. Further, that only 8 and 14 percent of these same respondents view themselves as conservative versus the 32 and 23 percent who view themselves as liberal.[12] Finally, even the press does not view itself accurate in presenting issues around religion. Only 13 percent of journalists and 18 percent of the public believe the press is accurate or very accurate in its coverage.[13] Should we expect anything else? At best they are the actions of Pharisees. At worst those supporting these ideas are turned from God and acting as part of a self-proclaimed elite. More on the elite and governance next.

Hold on to His Governance, No Matter What

Within pagan society, there is at least one elite faction that views itself as being most fit to rule, having the natural gift of leadership. *This view arises from the belief that all are not equal, but rather some are more equal than others.* They view their rule as fitting and just, that war is proper against all who do not submit. That sounds a lot to me like what we've seen play out not only recently, but growing over the last twenty-five years or so. Recent examples include the likes of Occupy Wall Street, Black Lives Matter, the Resist movement, and calls by at least one congressional representative to harass members of the current administration. These principles come directly from the works of Plato, Aristotle, and other pagan Greek philosophers.

Christianity asserts true leadership comes from within, and is earned by merit, based upon our actions. Leadership comes from within society, is recognized by society, and elected by society to serve society. This is demonstrated in the passage from Deuteronomy quoted earlier about the Israelites electing judges from within their own tribes and clans. These judges were to execute righteous justice, because the final judgement is God's.

Within pagan society, we again see a blending, this time one of power. Morality being defined by man, but just the elite, in the interest of the State, for the perpetuation of the State. Ideas again coming from pagan philosophy. *Within this line of thought, the people exist to serve the State.*

Christian thought again resolves this paradox by keeping the powers of morality and justice separate. *Morality is to be instilled in the people through their personal relationship with God. A personal relationship based upon love. This is the province of the Church.* Not all men subscribe to such thoughts, and some commit unjust acts such as murder, rape, and robbery. *Administering justice is the State's purpose, when individuals choose to act unjustly.* It is only earthly justice, one based upon actions as only God can see into other men's hearts. *Principles derived from Christianity assert that morality and justice are separate, both fully present, and both fully active at the same time.*

Enduring rights do not come from the State, but from God. His rights come to us through His words and actions; they convey His knowing and doing. Man can create rights, but those must not violate His commands for us. They can be additions to His will but are not to delete from it. They must promote virtue, including justice. Often man's rights do not promote justice. Take abortion. God's word states that one does not kill. However, *man grants the right of abortion as he concludes there is no life yet. There is no other species known in creation which holds that thought.* Life becomes a word devoid of value.

We know the difference between justice and injustice by the fruit a law bears. Does it lead to greater unity, peace, prosperity, and virtue as these things are from God? Or does it promote division, conflict, envy, and vice? The latter does not come from God, but man turned from Him, individuals choosing to do evil, man creating his own value for life, and over sixty million have died because of it.

Concluding Remarks

We are not defenseless in the face of evil. We are given the protection of the armor of God.[14] These metaphorical weapons include a breastplate, shield, helmet, sandals, and sword. They are effective weapons, but there is one thing to note about them. They are offensive weapons. They are only effective when advancing against the enemy. If one turns their back to the enemy, they lose their effectiveness. These weapons are intended to be used against those of this world who have given themselves to darkness, including rulers and those in authority. This battle is not ours to win or lose; we already know the story's end. Instead, we are called simply to stand for what is right and true.

Real truth is timeless; it does not change. We put God first. When we are obedient to His will, then everything else follows. When we are turned toward Him, we realize the benefits of the natural rights He's given us. We also have a duty to fulfill obligations that come with those rights, but those too are for our benefit. He's gifted us with these rights. It comes down to grace. It doesn't mean things will be easy, but we will never be alone, and with Him there will be nothing we face we cannot get through. The choice is always ours to make. So I'll end this book with the question that was the first book's premise: Do you want to be free?

Notes

CHAPTER 1

[1] Hamilton, Alexander, Madison, James, and Jay, John, p. 356, *The Federalist*, MetroBooks, 2002.
[2] West, Thomas G., p. 91, *The Political Theory of the American Founding*, Cambridge University Press, 2017.
[3] Evans, M. Stanton, p. 23, *The Theme is Freedom: Religion, Politics, and the American Tradition*, Regnery Publishing, 1994.
[4] Aquinas, St. Thomas, p. 109, *Summa Theologicæ*, Vol. 30, McGraw-Hill Publishing Co., 1970, Part 1a2ae, Question 110, Article 1. Future references to this work will denote the part, question, and article in the citation to make the passage easier to find.
[5] Genesis 1. All *Bible* citations come from the *New American Standard Bible*, unless otherwise noted.
[6] Lev. 11:44.
[7] Matt. 7:24-27.
[8] Augustine, p. 935, *City of God, Nicene and Post-Nicene Fathers*, Vol. II, Wm. B. Eerdmans Publishing Co., 1970. Book XIX, Chapter 14. Future references to this work will include the book and chapter in the citation.
[9] Augustine, p. 482, *The Enchiridion, Nicene and Post-Nicene Fathers*, Vol. III, Wm. B. Eerdmans Publishing Co., 1970. Chapter 3. Future references to this work will include the chapter number in the citation.
[10] Augustine, p. 1248, *Treatise on Grace and Free Will, Nicene and Post-Nicene Fathers*, Vol. V, Wm. B. Eerdmans Publishing Co., 1970. Chapter 21. Further references to this work will include the chapter number in the citation.
[11] Augustine, p. 483, *The Enchiridion, Nicene and Post-Nicene Fathers*, Vol. III, Wm. B. Eerdmans Publishing Co., 1970. Ch. 3.
[12] Ibid, p. 486.
[13] Augustine, p. 1239, *Treatise on Grace and Free Will, Nicene and Post-Nicene Fathers*, Vol. V, Wm. B. Eerdmans Publishing Co., 1970. Ch. 13.
[14] 1 Cor. 7:25, *Vulgate*.

[15] Augustine, p. 1239, *Treatise on Grace and Free Will, Nicene and Post-Nicene Fathers*, Vol. V, Wm. B. Eerdmans Publishing Co., 1970. Ch. 13.

[16] Augustine, p. 488, *The Enchiridion, Nicene and Post-Nicene Fathers*, Vol. III, Wm. B. Eerdmans Publishing Co., 1970. Chapter 8. The Bible quotation is Gal. 5:6.

[17] More information can be found in:
Model - Wolf, Dan, Chapter 1, *Collectivism and Charity*, living rightly publications, 2016.
Components - Wolf, Dan, Chapters, 3,4,and 5, *Do You Want To Be Free?*, Telemachus Press, 2013.

[18] Wolf, Dan, p. 202-228, *Do You Want To Be Free?*, Telemachus Press, 2013.

[19] Pew Research Center, *Religious Landscape Study*, May 12, 2015, http://www.pewforum.org/2015/05/12/americas-changing-religious-landscape/. Accessed March, 2018.

[20] Limbaugh, David, *Obama's Scandal-Free Delusion*, Townhall.com, March 2, 2018, at https://townhall.com/columnists/davidlimbaugh/2018/03/02/obamas-scandalfree-delusion-n2456233 is only one example. Accessed March, 2018.

[21] Deut. 6:4, Hear, O Israel! The Lord is our God, the Lord is one!
Matt. 28:18-20, And Jesus came up and spoke to them, saying, "All authority has been given to Me in heaven and on earth. Go therefore and make disciples of all the nations, baptizing them in the name of the Father and the Son and the Holy Spirit, teaching them to observe all that I commanded you; and lo, I am with you always, even to the end of the age."
John 1:1-3, In the beginning was the Word, and the Word was with God, and the Word was God. He was in the beginning with God. All things came into being through Him, and apart from Him nothing came into being that has come into being.

[22] Geisler, Norman L. and Saleeb, Abdul, p. 272, *Answering Islam*, Baker Books, 2008.

[23] Gross, T. (Host). (2014, April 10). Songwriters Behind 'Frozen' Let Go Of The Princess Mythology [Radio Broadcast episode]. https://www.npr.org/templates/transcript/transcript.php?storyId=301420227.

[24] Aquinas, St. Thomas, p. 11, *Summa Theologicæ*, Vol. 28, McGraw-Hill Publishing Co., 1970, Part 1a2ae, 90, 2.

[25] Ibid, Vol. 28, pp. 13-5, Part 1a2ae, 90, 3.

[26] Gratian, p. 4, *The Treatise on Laws,* The Catholic University of America Press, 1993.

[27] Aquinas, St. Thomas, pp. 19-21, *Summa Theologicæ*, Vol. 28, McGraw-Hill Publishing Co., 1970, Part 1a2ae, 91, 1.

[28] Ibid, Vol. 28, p. 57, Part 1a2ae, 93, 1.

[29] Ibid, Vol. 28, p. 59, Part 1a2ae, 93, 3.

[30] Ibid, Vol. 28. p. 63, Part 1a2ae, 93, 4.

[31] Gratian, p. 3, *The Treatise on Laws,* The Catholic University of America Press, 1993.
[32] Ibid, Vol. 28, p. 61, Part 1a2ae, 93, 3.
[33] Aquinas, St. Thomas, p. 124-5, *Summa Contra Gentiles*, Book III, Providence Part 2, Chapter 115.
[34] Aquinas, St. Thomas, p.29, *Summa Theologicæ*, Vol. 28, McGraw-Hill Publishing Co., 1970, Part 1a2ae, 91, 4.
[35] Ibid, Vol. 28, p. 23, Part 1a2ae, 91, 2.
[36] Ibid, Vol. 28, p. 81, Part 1a2ae, 94, 2.
[37] Ibid.
[38] Ibid, Vol. 28, p. 85, Part 1a2ae, 94, 3.
[39] Ibid, Vol. 16, pp 131-3. Part 1a2ae, 5, 5.
[40] Ibid, Vol. 28, pp. 87-9, Part 1a2ae, 94, 4.
[41] Ibid, Vol. 28, p. 97, Part 1a2ae, 94, 6.
[42] Ibid, Vol. 28, p. 155, Part 1a2ae, 97, 4.
[43] Ibid, Vol. 28, p. 93, Part 1a2ae, 94, 5.
[44] Ibid, Vol. 28, p. 105, Part 1a2ae, 95, 2.
[45] Ibid, Vol. 28, p. 109, Part 1a2ae, 95, 3.
[46] Ibid, Vol. 38, pp. 67-9, 2a2ae, 66, 2.
[47] Ibid, Vol. 28, p. 101, Part 1a2ae, 95, 1.
[48] Ibid, Vol. 28, p. 155, Part 1a2ae, 97, 4.
[49] Ibid, Vol. 28, p. 93, Part 1a2ae, 94, 5.
[50] Gratian, p. 29, *The Treatise on Laws,* The Catholic University of America Press, 1993.
[51] Beza, Theodore, *The Rights of Magistrates*, 1574, http://www.constitution.org/cmt/beza/magistrates.htm. Accessed May, 2018.
[52] Overton, Richard, *An Arrow Against All Tyrants and Tyranny*, 1646, http://oll.libertyfund.org/pages/overton-an-arrow-against-all-tyrants-1646. Accessed May, 2018.

CHAPTER 2

[1] Wolf, Dan, *Evil Raises Its Head Again*, http://www.livingrightly.net/Blog/tabid/87/ID/69/Evil-Raises-Its-Head-Again.aspx.
[2] Wolf, Dan, pp. 129-58, *Collectivism and Charity*, living rightly publications, 2016.

CHAPTER 3

[1] Galatians 5:19-23.
[2] Wolf, Dan, pp. 57-61, *Collectivism and Charity*, living rightly publications, 2016.

CHAPTER 4

[1] More on this topic can be found in Wolf, Dan, pp. 19-63, *Collectivism and Charity*, living rightly publications, 2016.

[2] Sheffield, Rachel and Rector, Robert, *Understanding Poverty in the United States: Surprising Facts About America's Poor*, The Heritage Foundation, 9/13/2011. At: https://www.heritage.org/poverty-and-inequality/report/understanding-poverty-the-united-states-surprising-facts-about, accessed 7/2018.

[3] Randolph, Erik, p. 26, *Modeling Potential Income and Welfare-Assistance Benefits in Illinois*, Illinois Policy Institute, December, 2014. At: https://d2dv7hze646xr.cloudfront.net/wp-content/uploads/2014/12/Welfare_Report_finalfinal.pdf. Accessed 07/2018.

[4] Noss, Amanda, *Household Income: 2013*, U.S. Census Bureau, September, 2014. At: https://www.census.gov/content/dam/Census/library/publications/2014/acs/acsbr13-02.pdf. Accessed, 07/2018.

[5] Wolf, Dan, pp. 172-83, *Collectivism and Charity*, living rightly publications, 2016.

[6] Wolf, Dan, pp. 230-51, *Do You Want to Be Free?* Telemachus Press, 2013.

[7] Ibid.

[8] Edwards, Jonathan, p. 37, *The Works of Jonathan Edwards*, Vol. 2, Hendrickson Publishers, 2006.

CHAPTER 5

[1] More about the interfaith movement in this context can be found in Wolf, Dan, *Coexist: Interfaith Myth and Misinformation*, Virginia Christian Alliance, 2017. Much of this book's contents can also be read at http://www.vachristian.org/Board-of-Advisors/Dan-Wolf.html.

[2] Wolf, Dan, pp. 8-9, *Charity and Collectivism*, living rightly publications, 2016.

[3] Ibid, pp. viii-xi.

[4] Charities Aid Foundation, *The World Giving Index 2010* and *CAF World Giving Index 2017*, at https://www.cafonline.org/about-us/publications. Accessed 7/2018.

[5] Brooks, Arthur C., *Who Really Cares*, Basic Books, 2006.

[6] Ibid, p. 32.

[7] Much of this section's contents comes from Wolf, Dan, *Coexist*, Virginia Christian Alliance, 2017.

[8] Warren, Rick, p. 149, *The Purpose Driven Life: What On Earth Am I Here For?* Zondervan, 2012.

[9] Chesterton, G.K., p. 65, *Orthodoxy*, Jefferson Publications, 2015.

[10] Roberts, Alexander, Rev, and Donaldson, James, p. 225, *The Ante-Nicene Fathers, Fathers of the Second Century: Hermas, Tatian, Athenagora,*

Theophilus, and Clement of Alexandria (Entire), Vol. 2, Wm. B Eerdmans Publishing Co., 1989. Paedagogus, Book I, Chapter VIII.

[11] Chesterton, G.K., p. 49, *Orthodoxy*, Jefferson Publications, 2015.

[12] *State of the Media*, Pew Research Center, Washington, D.C. (February, 2011). http://www.stateofthemedia.org/files/2011/02/Journalists-topline.pdf. Accessed 8/2018.

[13] *Americans and the News Media: What they do—and don't—understand about each other*, Pew Research Center, Washington, D.C. (June, 2018). https://www.americanpressinstitute.org/wp-content/uploads/2018/06/Americans-and-the-News-Media-2018.pdf. Accessed 8/2018.

[14] See Ephesians 6:10-17, Finally, be strong in the Lord and in his mighty power. Put on the full armor of God, so that you can take your stand against the devil's schemes. For our struggle is not against flesh and blood, but against the rulers, against the authorities, against the powers of this dark world and against the spiritual forces of evil in the heavenly realms. Therefore put on the full armor of God, so that when the day of evil comes, you may be able to stand your ground, and after you have done everything, to stand. Stand firm then, with the belt of truth buckled around your waist, with the breastplate of righteousness in place, and with your feet fitted with the readiness that comes from the gospel of peace. In addition to all this, take up the shield of faith, with which you can extinguish all the flaming arrows of the evil one. Take the helmet of salvation and the sword of the Spirit, which is the word of God.